California Treasures

Writing and Grammar

TEACHER'S EDITION

Macmillan/McGraw-Hill

The *McGraw·Hill* Companies   B

 Macmillan/McGraw-Hill

Published by Macmillan/McGraw-Hill, of McGraw-Hill Education, a division of The McGraw-Hill Companies, Inc., Two Penn Plaza, New York, New York 10121.

Printed in the United States of America

5 6 7 8 9 10 MAL 11

Table of Contents

Linguistic Differences (AAVE)
Section 1   2

Grammar: Nouns, Verbs, and Complete Sentences
Section 2   26

Grammar: Kinds of Sentences
Section 3   46

Grammar: Nouns, Pronouns, and Subject-Verb Agreement
Section 4   62

Grammar: Verb Tenses and Contractions
Section 5   82

Grammar: Adjectives and Adverbs
Section 6   **102**

Grammar: Possessives and Proper Nouns
Section 7   **116**

Writing: Letter, Invitation, and Thank-You Note
Section 8   **130**

Writing: Description
Section 9   148

Writing: Autobiographical Narrative
Section 10   168

© Macmillan/McGraw-Hill

Writing: Fictional Narrative
Section 11 190

Writing: Informational Paragraph
Section 12 208

Using *Grammar and Writing Intervention*

Purpose and Use

California Treasures provides a set of strategic intervention materials, one set for each of the key technical skill domains of beginning reading (phonemic awareness and phonological awareness, phonics and decoding, oral reading fluency, vocabulary, and reading comprehension skills) plus writing and grammar. Each set of materials contains over ninety 15-minute lessons. These lessons

- focus on children in Kindergarten through Grade 3 who need reteaching and practice in one or more of the technical skill domains;
- provide explicit, sequential, and systematic needs-based instruction of standards taught in the target grade or previous grade;
- are connected to the basic program and consistent with the key instructional routines used;
- are designed for efficient and effective use in tutorial or small-group instructional settings;
- can be administered by a teacher or teacher's aide but are also great for after-school programs and one-on-one tutoring sessions;
- contain a periodic progress-monitoring assessment for determining attainment of skills taught after approximately every ten lessons.

Contents and Resources

Grammar and Writing Intervention organizes instruction and practice on two-page spreads for ease of use. A short, 15-minute lesson provides targeted instruction in a discrete skill. A Practice Reproducible provides targeted practice for that skill. Lessons are grouped into three kinds of sections:

- Linguistic Differences (support for speakers of African American Vernacular)
- Grammar
- Writing

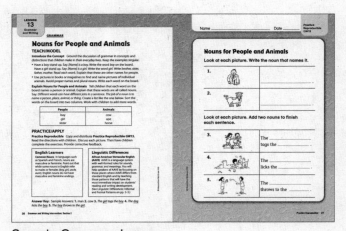

Sample Grammar Lesson

Assessment

Placement To place children in the *Grammar and Writing Intervention* scope and sequence, use the *Analytic Writing Assessment* in the **Diagnostic Assessment.** Developed by program author Doug Fisher, this test determines general areas of writing weakness. Children can also be placed in the sequence of lessons based on a lack of mastery of grammar and writing skills in the core program.

Each section focuses on a small set of grammar or writing skills. You can place children in the following ways:

Diagnostic Assessment

- You can teach a discrete lesson or a discrete group of lessons as a prescription for specific skills that children have not yet mastered.

- You can provide sequential and systematic instruction over a longer period of time, perhaps as a regular part of additional instruction that you might be providing a group of struggling readers.

Progress Monitoring To determine children's mastery of skills taught, use the progress-monitoring assessment provided at the end of each section. These assessments appear after about every ten lessons. Use the results to determine which children are ready to move on and which need to repeat the sequence of lessons. (See below for samples of the two kinds of assessments used in *Grammar and Writing Intervention*.)

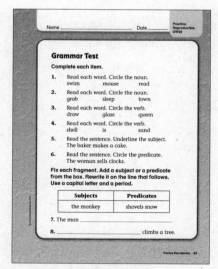

Sample Grammar Test

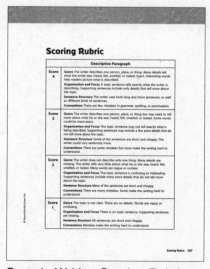

Sample Writing Scoring Rubric

- In Section 1–Section 7, a formal assessment supports progress monitoring. Each assessment measures mastery of the discrete skills taught in that section.
- In Section 8–Section 12, a scoring rubric supports progress monitoring. Each rubric is designed to be used with the independent writing that children do in that section.

Instructional Routines

Highly explicit and narrow in focus, each section of *Grammar and Writing Intervention* builds slowly from foundational skills, following a scope and sequence that is consistent with the *California Treasures* core program. Lessons use routines for explicit instruction and teacher modeling, as well as guided and independent practice, that are also consistent with the core program.

Instructional Modifications

Most struggling readers will also struggle with grammar and writing in the core program. These children need more time and practice to master foundational skills. The lessons in *Grammar and Writing Intervention* are ideal for these children.

- Speakers of African American Vernacular English (AAVE) may have difficulty learning the rules of standard English. For these children, consider teaching some or all of the lessons in Section 1: Linguistic Differences. Grammar lessons in Section 2–Section 7 provide additional support for AAVE speakers.
- English learners may also require more time and instruction. Grammar lessons in Section 2–Section 7 provide additional support for these children. These children will also benefit from the targeted writing instruction and scaffolded practice in Section 8–Section 12.

Research and Guiding Principles

Linguistic Differences Some of your children will be speakers of African American Vernacular English (AAVE). AAVE is a language system with well-formed rules for sounds, grammar, and meanings. Research has shown that teaching these children to switch back and forth between AAVE and the rules of standard English can immediately benefit their reading and writing development. Section 1 teaches this kind of "code switching," using contrastive analysis exercises that identify systematic differences between standard and nonstandard English while still respecting children's home language.

Grammar Formal grammar instruction is more effective the more closely it can be connected with children's authentic efforts to communicate their thoughts and ideas. In Section 2–Section 7, grammar principles are often introduced orally, and practice for each lesson applies the skill to a short, open-ended writing activity. Lessons progress in difficulty very slowly, initially using only singular nouns and present tense verbs. Spiral review is integrated into many lessons, supporting the mastery of important grammar skills such as using subject-verb agreement, forming complete sentences, and applying correct capitalization and punctuation.

Writing Young writers need explicit instruction in the stages of the writing process—in particular, prewriting, drafting, and revising. Research indicates that children also benefit from lessons in writing strategies that can be used at each stage of the writing process, such as organization and sentence combining. Children also write more effectively when they can discuss their work at each stage of the process. Conversations about prewriting, drafting, and revising deepen young writers' understanding of audience and purpose. In Section 8–Section 12, Genre Features lessons use multiple models to introduce the criteria for each genre and clarify academic language. Writing Strategies lessons target genre-related skills such as using time order, adding details, and writing topic sentences. Writing Applications lessons use partner activities, sentence frames, and highly structured graphic organizers to scaffold children's independent writing.

LINGUISTIC DIFFERENCES

Informal and Formal Patterns

TEACH/MODEL

Understanding Linguistic Differences   Some children will be speakers of African American Vernacular English (AAVE). These children will need help understanding that what is appropriate in one setting is not appropriate in another, so they can shift easily and competently between varieties of English in different social contexts. Instruction will be more effective if it identifies non-standard varieties of English as different, rather than inferior. All children should be taught standard English in a way that respects their home language.

Introduce Informal and Formal Social Contexts   Use kinds of clothing to help children understand the differences between formal and informal social contexts.

- Ask: *What places do you go where you wear play clothes that can get dirty?* List some examples on the board. If children need prompting, suggest the following: a playground, the park, a friend's house.

- Ask: *What places do you go where you have to wear nice clothes that you try to keep clean?* List some examples on the board. If children need prompting, suggest the following: school, church, Grandma's house for a holiday meal.

- Sort examples into a chart like the one shown below.

Informal	Formal
playground	school
friend's house	church
the park	Grandma's house

Discuss Linguistic Differences   Explain that just as people dress differently to go different places, they can also speak differently. Say: *Just like they have play clothes and fancy clothes, people also have different ways of speaking.* **Informal English** is the way we speak with family and friends. **Standard English,** also called **formal English,** is the way we speak in more formal settings, such as school.

PRACTICE/APPLY

Practice Reproducible   Copy and distribute **Practice Reproducible GW1.** Read the directions and the sentences with children. Have partners sort examples into the two columns. Then have them write their own examples in the boxes at the bottom. Provide corrective feedback. Discuss answers as a group.

Answer Key: Informal *the beach, baseball game, cookout, sleepover*
Formal *church, wedding, school, fancy restaurant*

Informal and Formal Patterns

Work with a partner. Read each example below. Then cut out the boxes and sort each example. Finally, work together to write your own examples in the boxes at the bottom.

Informal		Formal	

_____		_____	
_____		_____	

✂

the beach	baseball game
wedding	church
cookout	sleepover
school	fancy restaurant

Possessive Patterns ('s)

TEACH/MODEL

Introduce the Concept   Ground the discussion in familiar concepts. Accept all responses, including African American Vernacular English. Don't correct children or comment on linguistic differences until the second half of this lesson.

- Say: *We own things. We own toys, books, clothes.* Point at something a child is wearing. Ask: *Whose shirt is this?* Accept both *Joe shirt* and *Joe's shirt*. Repeat answers exactly as children say them, and write one or two on the board.

- Say: *We have hands, feet, noses, faces.* Point at a child's hand. Ask: *Whose hand is this?* Accept both *Jilian's hand* and *Jilian hand*. Repeat and write answers.

- Say: *We have mothers, fathers, brothers, sisters.* Using the names of children in the group, write examples such as *Nico's dad* on the board. Have children repeat.

Discuss Linguistic Differences   Now guide speakers of African American Vernacular English to contrast how the possessive is formed in informal English with how it is formed in formal English, also called standard English. Help them to recognize and analyze the pattern of differences.

- Say: *In formal English, you use an apostrophe and an* s *('s) to show ownership.* Point at an example on the board. *Nico's mom.* Have children repeat. Circle the *'s.*

- Say: *When you speak, you might not always use the possessive.* Point at another example on the board: *Jilian hand.* Have children repeat it.

- Then start a chart like the one shown below. Sort the phrases on the board. Then have children supply examples so every phrase is shown in both informal English and formal English. Correct errors in how children sort phrases.

Informal English	Formal English
Joe shirt	Joe's shirt
Jilian hand	Jilian's hand
Nico mom	Nico's mom

PRACTICE/APPLY

Practice Reproducible   Copy and distribute **Practice Reproducible GW2.** Read the text with children. Have partners sort phrases into the columns and write their own examples. Provide corrective feedback. Discuss answers as a group.

Answer Key: Informal *boy coat, Rick hat, Mom job, Keisha brother, dog nose*
Formal *boy<u>'s</u> coat, Rick<u>'s</u> hat, Mom<u>'s</u> job, Keisha<u>'s</u> brother, dog<u>'s</u> nose*

Possessive Patterns ('s)

Work with a partner. Read each example below.
Circle every 's. Then cut out the boxes and sort
each example. Finally, work together to write your
own examples in the boxes at the bottom.

Informal	Formal

_____	_____
_____	_____

boy coat	Mom's job
Rick's hat	Keisha's brother
Keisha brother	dog nose
Rick hat	boy's coat
dog's nose	Mom job

<u>LINGUISTIC DIFFERENCES</u>

Plural Patterns

TEACH/MODEL

Introduce the Concept Ground the discussion in familiar concepts. Accept all responses, including African American Vernacular English (AAVE). Don't correct children or comment on linguistic differences until the second half of the lesson.

- Say: *When we speak or write about more than one, we use words to tell that we mean more than one.* Have a child hold up both hands. Ask: *How many fingers does [name] have?* Accept both *Amy has ten finger* and *Amy has ten fingers*. Repeat answers exactly as children say them. Write one or two on the board.

- Have a child count the pencils in his or her desk. Ask: *How many pencils does [name] have?* Accept both *Andre has three pencil* and *Andre has three pencils*. Repeat answers, and write them on the board. Continue this routine with other items.

Discuss Linguistic Differences Guide speakers of AAVE to contrast how the plural is formed in informal English and formal English, also called standard English. Help them to recognize and analyze the pattern of differences.

- Say: *In formal English, you add an* s *to show more than one.* Point to an example on the board: *Jimar wears two shoes.* Have children repeat. Circle the *s*. Say: *When you speak, you might not always add the* s. Point to another example on the board: *Amy has ten finger*. Have children repeat.

- Then start a chart like the one shown below. Sort the phrases on the board. Then have children supply examples so every phrase is shown in both informal English and formal English. Correct errors in how children sort phrases.

Informal English	Formal English
Amy has ten finger.	Amy has ten fingers.
Andre has two pencil.	Andre has two pencils.
Angela has three book.	Angela has three books.

PRACTICE/APPLY

Practice Reproducible Copy and distribute **Practice Reproducible GW3.** Read the text with children. Have partners sort sentences into the columns and write their own examples. Provide corrective feedback. Discuss answers as a group.

Answer Key: Informal *Delmar has two dog. Three cat ran away. We saw five kite. One of my hat is red. We saw five car* **Formal** *Delmar has two dogs. Three cats ran away. We saw five kites. One of my hats is red. We saw five cars.*

Plural Patterns

Work with a partner. Read each example below. Circle every *s* that means more than one. Then cut out the boxes and sort each example. Finally, work together to write your own examples in the boxes at the bottom.

Informal	Formal
_____	_____

✂

Delmar has two dog.	One of my hat is red.
Three cats ran away.	We saw five cars.
We saw five kite.	Three cat ran away.
One of my hats is red.	We saw five kites.
We saw five car.	Delmar has two dogs.

Past Tense Patterns

TEACH/MODEL

Introduce the Concept   Ground the discussion in familiar concepts. Accept all responses, including African American Vernacular English (AAVE). Don't correct children or comment on linguistic differences until the second half of the lesson.

- Say: *When we speak or write about the past, we use verbs that show that something has happened already.* Ask: *What did you do at recess yesterday?* Accept both *Yesterday I play tag* and *Yesterday I played tag.* Repeat and write answers exactly as children say them, avoiding examples with irregular verbs such as *saw* and *ran.*

- Say: *[Name], when in the past did you listen to music?* Accept both *Last week I listen to music* and *Last week I listened to music.* Repeat and write the answers.

- Say: *We did lots of things in the past.* Using the names of children in the group, write examples such as *Brianna jumped rope* on the board. Have children repeat.

Discuss Linguistic Differences   Now guide speakers of AAVE to contrast how the past tense is formed in informal English and formal English, also called standard English. Help them recognize and analyze the pattern of differences.

- Say: In formal English, you often add the letters *ed* to show past tense. Point to an example on the board: *Last week I listened to music.* Have children repeat. Circle the *ed.* Say: *When you speak, you might not always add the* ed. Point to another example on the board: *Last week I listen to music.* Have children repeat.

- Then start a chart like the one shown below. Sort the phrases on the board. Then have children supply examples so every phrase is shown in both informal English and formal English. Correct errors in how children sort phrases.

Informal English	Formal English
Last week I listen to music.	Last week I listened to music.
Yesterday I play tag.	Yesterday I played tag.
Brianna jump rope.	Brianna jumped rope.

PRACTICE/APPLY

Practice Reproducible   Copy and distribute **Practice Reproducible GW4.** Read the text with children. Have partners sort sentences into the columns and write their own examples. Provide corrective feedback. Discuss answers as a group.

Answer Key: Informal *We play last night. Yesterday Lee visit. You skate last year. Last Friday I shop. I fish once before.* **Formal** *We played last night. Yesterday Lee visited. You skated last year. Last Friday I shopped. I fished once before.*

Past Tense Patterns

Work with a partner. Read each example below. Circle every *ed* that means past tense. Then cut out the boxes and sort each example. Finally, work together to write your own examples in the boxes at the bottom.

Informal	Formal
_____	_____

✂ -

We played last night.	You skated last year.
Yesterday Lee visit.	Last Friday I shopped.
You skate last year.	I fished once before.
Yesterday Lee visited.	We play last night.
Last Friday I shop.	I fish once before.

<u>**LINGUISTIC DIFFERENCES**</u>

Using *is* and *are*

TEACH/MODEL

Introduce the Concept Ground the discussion in familiar concepts. Accept all responses, including African American Vernacular English (AAVE). Don't correct children or comment on linguistic differences until the second half of the lesson.

- Say: *Many of us have brothers and sisters.* Supply this example, using a member of your family: *[Name] is my brother/sister.* Write it on the board. Say: *Tell me the name of someone in your family and tell how that person is related to you.* Accept both *Antoine is my brother* as well as both *Antoine my brother* and *Antoine be my brother.* Repeat and write answers on the board exactly as children say them.

- Say: *Name one thing in the room and say what color it is.* Accept *This pencil is yellow* as well as both *This pencil yellow* and *This pencil be yellow.* Say answers aloud and write them. Repeat the process with a plural noun: *The tables are large.*

Discuss Linguistic Differences Now guide speakers of AAVE to contrast how formal English, or standard English, uses *is* and *are* while informal English often leaves them out. Help them to recognize the pattern of differences.

- Say: *In formal English, you use* is *and* are *when you describe someone or something.* Point to an example on the board: *Antoine is my brother* and *The tables are large.* Have children repeat. Circle *is* and *are.* Say: *When you speak, you might not always use* is *and* are. Repeat with other examples on the board.

- Then start a chart like the one shown below. Sort the phrases on the board. Then have children supply examples so every phrase is shown in both informal English and formal English. Correct errors in how children sort phrases.

Informal English	Formal English
Antoine my brother.	Antoine is my brother.
This pencil be yellow.	This pencil is yellow.
The tables be large.	The tables are large.

PRACTICE/APPLY

Practice Reproducible Copy and distribute **Practice Reproducible GW5.** Read the text with children. Have partners sort sentences into the columns and write their own examples. Provide corrective feedback. Discuss answers as a group.

Answer Key: Informal *My shoes blue. That bed be soft. Gracie my sister. Those trees tall. Baseball be fun* **Formal** *My shoes <u>are</u> blue. That bed <u>is</u> soft. Gracie <u>is</u> my sister. Those trees <u>are</u> tall. Baseball <u>is</u> fun.*

Practice
Reproducible
GW5

Using *is* and *are*

Work with a partner. Read each example below. Circle *is* and *are*. Then cut out the boxes and sort each example. Finally, work together to write your own examples in the boxes at the bottom.

Informal	Formal

My shoes are blue.	Those trees are tall.
That bed be soft.	Baseball be fun.
Gracie my sister.	My shoes blue.
Those trees tall.	That bed is soft.
Baseball is fun.	Gracie is my sister.

LINGUISTIC DIFFERENCES

Subject-Verb Agreement (Regular Verbs)

TEACH/MODEL

Introduce the Concept   Ground the discussion in familiar concepts. Accept all responses, including African American Vernacular English (AAVE). Don't correct children or comment on linguistic differences until the second half of the lesson.

- Have a child raise his or her hand. Ask: *If I ask a question, what does [name] do?* Accept both *Jared raise hand* and *Jared raises his hand.* Have children perform other actions. Ask them to dictate sentences about the actions. Accept both *Robert talk* and *Robert talks.* Repeat answers, and write them on the board.

- Say: *We do lots of active things.* Supply these examples, using the names of children in the group: *Takeisha draws a picture. Stella leads a band.* Write these examples on the board. Have children repeat them.

Discuss Linguistic Differences   Guide speakers of AAVE to contrast subject-verb agreement in informal English and formal, or standard, English. Help them recognize and analyze the pattern of differences. Conjugate the verb *to raise.*

- Say: *In formal English, you add an* s *to the action verb when only one person does the action.* Point to an example on the board: *Jared raises his hand.* Have children repeat. Circle the *s.* Say: *When you speak, you might not always add the* s. Point to another example on the board: *Robert talk.* Have children repeat.

- Start a chart like the one below. Sort phrases and have children supply examples so every phrase is shown in both informal and formal English. Correct errors.

Informal English	Formal English
Jared raise his hand.	Jared raises his hand.
Robert talk.	Robert talks.
Takeisha draw a picture.	Takeisha draws a picture.

PRACTICE/APPLY

Practice Reproducible   Copy and distribute **Practice Reproducible GW6.** Read the text with children. Have partners sort sentences into columns and write their own examples. Provide corrective feedback. Discuss answers as a group.

Answer Key: Informal *Dad sing a song. Joy color a picture. Keisha win a race. Turell clean his bike. The pony run fast.* **Formal** *Dad sings a song. Joy colors a picture. Keisha wins a race. Turell cleans his bike. The pony runs fast.*

Subject-Verb Agreement
(Regular Verbs)

Work with a partner. Read each example below.
Circle every *s* added to a verb. Then cut out the
boxes and sort each example. Finally, work
together to write your own examples in the boxes
at the bottom.

Informal	Formal

_____	_____

✂

Dad sings a song.	Turell cleans his bike.
Joy color a picture.	Keisha wins a race.
Keisha win a race.	The pony run fast.
Turell clean his bike.	Joy colors a picture.
The pony runs fast.	Dad sing a song.

Subject-Verb Agreement (*is/are, was/were*)

TEACH/MODEL

Introduce the Concept   Ground the discussion in familiar concepts. Accept all responses, including African American Vernacular English (AAVE). Don't correct children or comment on linguistic differences until the second half of the lesson.

- Ask: *Who is here today?* Accept both *We is here today* and *We are here today*. Repeat answers exactly as children say them, and write one or two on the board.

- Supply more examples, using names of children in the group: *Sara and Devon were listening. Jack and Mark were running.* Write them and have children repeat.

Discuss Linguistic Differences   Guide speakers of AAVE to contrast subject-verb agreement in informal English and formal English, also called standard English. Help them to recognize and analyze the pattern of differences.

- Conjugate the verb *to be* on the board. Write *I am, she is, he is, we are, they are* for the present and *I was, he was, she was, we were, they were* for the past. Read the phrases together with children. Say: *In formal English, you use* is/are *and* was/were. Then point to an example: *We are here today*. Have children repeat. Circle *are*. Point to the conjugation of the verb *to be*. Ask: *Does this kind of English use* is *or* are *with* I? *with* we? *with* she? *with* he? *with* they? Repeat with *was* and *were*.

- Say: *When you speak, you might not always use* am, is, are, was, *and* were. Point to another example on the board: *We is here today*. Have children repeat. Start a chart like the one below. Sort phrases and have children supply examples so every phrase is shown in both informal and formal English. Correct errors.

Informal English	Formal English
We is here today.	We are here today.
Jack and Mark was running.	Jack and Mark were running.
Sara and Devon was listening.	Sara and Devon were listening.

PRACTICE/APPLY

Practice Reproducible   Copy and distribute **Practice Reproducible GW7.** Read the text with children. Have partners sort sentences into columns and write their own examples. Provide corrective feedback. Discuss answers as a group.

Answer Key: Informal *We was singing. You was mad. They is coming. We is home. We was late.* **Formal** *We were singing. You were mad. They are coming. We are home. We were late.*

Practice
Reproducible
GW7

Subject-Verb Agreement
(*is/are, was/were*)

Work with a partner. Read each example below.
Circle *is, are, was,* and *were.* Then cut out the
boxes and sort each example. Finally, work
together to write your own examples in the boxes
at the bottom.

Informal	Formal

_____	_____

✂

We was singing.	We was late.
You was mad.	We are home.
They are coming.	They is coming.
We is home.	You were mad.
We were late.	We were singing.

LINGUISTIC DIFFERENCES

Subject-Verb Agreement (do/does, have/has)

TEACH/MODEL

Introduce the Concept   Ground the discussion in familiar concepts. Accept all responses, including African American Vernacular English (AAVE). Don't correct children or comment on linguistic differences until the second half of the lesson.

- Say: *Who does well in school?* Accept both *Kim do well in school* and *Kim does well in school*. Repeat answers exactly as children say them, and write one or two on the board. Continue with other questions, such as *Who does well at sports?*

- Ask: *Who has a pencil?* Accept both *Lucas have a pencil* and *Lucas has a pencil*. Repeat answers, and write one or two. Using names in the group, supply other examples such as: *Leonda has a nice hat*. Write them and have children repeat.

Discuss Linguistic Differences   Guide speakers of AAVE to contrast verb forms in informal and formal English, recognizing and analyzing the pattern of differences.

- Conjugate the verb *to do*. Write and read aloud *I do, she does, he does, we do, they do*. Repeat with *to have*. Say: *In formal English, you use* do/does *and* has/have. Point to examples: *Kim does well at school* and *Leonda has a nice hat*. Have children repeat. Circle *does* and *has*. Then point to the conjugations. Ask: *Does this kind of English use* do *or* does *with* I? *with* we? *with* she? *with* he? *with* they? Repeat with *has/have*.

- Say: *When you speak, you might not always use the same verb form*. Point to *Kim do well in school*. Have children repeat. Start a chart like the one below. Sort phrases and have children supply examples so every phrase is shown in both informal English and in formal English. Correct errors.

Informal English	Formal English
Kim do well at school.	Kim does well at school.
Lucas have a pencil.	Lucas has a pencil.
Leonda have a nice hat.	Leonda has a nice hat.

PRACTICE/APPLY

Practice Reproducible   Copy and distribute **Practice Reproducible GW8.** Read the text with children. Have partners work together to sort sentences into columns and write their own examples. Provide corrective feedback and discuss answers.

Answer Key: Informal *Marcus <u>do</u> a good job. We <u>has</u> two keys. They <u>has</u> the toys. The runner <u>do</u> well. Latitia <u>have</u> a new coat.* **Formal** *Marcus <u>does</u> a good job. We <u>have</u> two keys. They <u>have</u> the toys. The runner <u>does</u> well. Latitia <u>has</u> a new coat.*

Subject-Verb Agreement
(*do/does, have/has*)

Work with a partner. Read each example below.
Circle *do*, *does*, *have*, and *has*. Then cut out
the boxes and sort each example. Finally, work
together to write your own examples in the boxes
at the bottom.

Informal	Formal

_____

_____

✂ -

Marcus do a good job.	The runner do well.
We has two keys.	Marcus does a good job.
They has the toys.	Latitia have a new coat.
The runner does well.	They have the toys.
Latitia has a new coat.	We have two keys.

LINGUISTIC DIFFERENCES

Possessive Patterns (who/whose)

TEACH/MODEL

Introduce the Concept   Ground the discussion in familiar concepts. Accept all responses, including African American Vernacular English (AAVE). Don't correct children or comment on linguistic differences until the second half of the lesson.

- Have children close their eyes. Borrow a pencil from one child, and place it on the desk of another. Guide the child who now has the pencil to ask whose pencil it is. Accept both *Who pencil is this?* and *Whose pencil is this?* Repeat answers exactly as children say them, and write one or two on the board. Continue with other objects, such as books.

- Using other objects that children in your group have, supply examples such as *I know whose jacket this is.* Write the examples and have children repeat them.

Discuss Linguistic Differences   Guide speakers of AAVE to contrast *who* in informal English and *whose* in formal English, also called standard English. Help them recognize and analyze the pattern of differences.

- Say: *In formal English, the word* whose *shows ownership.* Point to an example on the board: *Whose book is this?* Have children repeat. Circle the word *whose*.

- Say: *When you speak, you might not always use the word* whose. Point to another example on the board: *Who pencil is this?* Have children repeat.

- Start a chart like the one shown below. Sort the phrases on the board. Then have children supply examples so every phrase is shown in both informal English and formal English. Correct errors in how children sort phrases.

Informal English	Formal English
Who pencil is this?	Whose pencil is this?
Who book is this?	Whose book is this?
I know who jacket this is.	I know whose jacket this is.

PRACTICE/APPLY

Practice Reproducible   Copy and distribute **Practice Reproducible GW9.** Read the text with children. Then have partners sort sentences and write their own examples. Provide corrective feedback. Discuss answers as a group.

Answer Key: Informal *Who red coat is this? Who hat is blue? Who ticket was lost? I know who glove that is. Who backpack is that?* **Formal** *Whose red coat is this? Whose hat is blue? Whose ticket was lost? I know whose glove that is. Whose backpack is that?*

© Macmillan/McGraw-Hill

Possessive Patterns (*who/whose*)

Work with a partner. Read each example below.
Circle the word *whose*. Then cut out the boxes and
sort each example. Finally, work together to write
your own examples in the boxes at the bottom.

Informal	Formal
_____	_____

✂

Whose red coat is this?	Who backpack is that?
Who hat is blue?	Whose ticket was lost?
Who ticket was lost?	Whose hat is blue?
Whose backpack is that?	Who red coat is this?
I know whose glove that is.	I know who glove that is.

<u>LINGUISTIC DIFFERENCES</u>

Habitual *be*

TEACH/MODEL

Introduce the Concept   Ground the discussion in familiar concepts. Accept all responses, including African American Vernacular English (AAVE). Don't correct children or comment on linguistic differences until the second half of the lesson.

- Guide children to make statements about things they wear every day. Accept both *I be wearing glasses* and *I always wear glasses*. Repeat answers exactly as children say them, and write one or two on the board.

- Guide children to make statements about things they do in the classroom every day. Accept both *We be reading* and *We usually read*. Repeat answers exactly, and write one or two. Using the names of children in the group, supply examples such as *Amy usually carries a backpack*. Write the examples. Have children repeat.

Discuss Linguistic Differences   Now guide speakers of AAVE to contrast how informal English uses *be* when formal, or standard, English might use *always* or *usually*. Help them recognize and analyze the pattern of differences.

- Say: *In formal English, people use words such as* always *or* usually *to talk about things we do every day*. Point to these examples: *I always wear glasses* and *Amy usually carries a backpack*. Have children repeat. Circle *usually* and *always*.

- Say: *When you speak, you might use* be *instead of words such as* always *and* usually. Point to an example: *I be wearing glasses*. Have children repeat it. Then start a chart like the one below. Sort phrases and have children supply examples so every phrase is shown in both informal and formal English. Correct errors.

Informal English	Formal English
I be wearing glasses.	I always wear glasses.
We be reading.	We usually read.
Amy be carrying a backpack.	Amy usually carries a backpack.

PRACTICE/APPLY

Practice Reproducible   Copy and distribute **Practice Reproducible GW10.** Read the text with children. Have partners sort sentences into the columns and write their own examples. Provide corrective feedback. Discuss answers as a group.

Answer Key: Informal *She <u>be</u> walking home. We <u>be</u> eating lunch here. Lin <u>be</u> talking on the phone. Shona <u>be</u> riding her bike. They <u>be</u> taking the bus.* **Formal** *She <u>usually</u> walks home. We <u>usually</u> eat lunch here. Lin <u>usually</u> talks on the phone. Shona <u>always</u> rides her bike. They <u>always</u> take the bus.*

Habitual *be*

Work with a partner. Read each example below.
Circle the words *be*, *always*, and *usually*. Then
cut out the boxes and sort each example. Finally,
work together to write your own examples in the
boxes at the bottom.

Informal
_____

Formal
_____

✂

She be walking home.	Shona always rides her bike.
We usually eat lunch now.	They be taking the bus.
Lin be talking on the phone.	She usually walks home.
Shona be riding her bike.	They always take the bus.
Lin usually talks on the phone.	We be eating lunch now.

<u>LINGUISTIC DIFFERENCES</u>

Patterns with Negatives

TEACH/MODEL

Introduce the Concept   Ground the discussion in familiar concepts. Accept all responses, including African American Vernacular English (AAVE). Don't correct children or comment on linguistic differences until the second half of the lesson.

- Ask: *Does a turtle have any wings?* Accept both *A turtle don't have no wings* and *A turtle doesn't have any wings.* Repeat answers exactly and write one or two.

- Write these examples: *Nobody never said nothing* and *Nobody ever said anything; They don't let nobody run* and *They don't let anybody run.* Have children repeat.

Discuss Linguistic Differences   Now guide speakers of AAVE to contrast how negatives are used in informal English and formal English, also called standard English. Help them recognize and analyze the pattern of differences.

- Explain that a negative is a word such as *no, not, nothing,* or *nobody.* Remind children that contractions such as *isn't, don't,* and *aren't* are also negatives. Say: *In formal English, a sentence has just one negative word. It might also have a word such as* any *or* ever. Point to an example: *A turtle doesn't have any wings.* Have children repeat. Underline the negative word. Circle *any.*

- Say: *When you speak, you might use more than one negative word. You might also not use words such as* any *or* ever. Point to another example: *A turtle don't have no wings.* Have children repeat. Circle the negative words. Then start a chart like the one below. Sort the phrases and have children supply examples so every phrase is shown in both informal and formal English. Correct errors.

Informal English	Formal English
A turtle don't have no wings.	A turtle doesn't have any wings.
Nobody never said nothing.	Nobody ever said anything.
They don't let nobody run.	They don't let anybody run.

PRACTICE/APPLY

Practice Reproducible   Copy and distribute **Practice Reproducible GW11.** Read the text with children. Have partners sort sentences into columns and write their own examples. Provide corrective feedback and discuss answers.

Answer Key: Informal *Nobody never did nothing. I don't like no other team. They didn't let nobody play. She won't never come. He doesn't want no pie.* **Formal** *Nobody ever did anything. I don't like any other team. They didn't let anybody play. She won't ever come. He doesn't want any pie.*

Patterns with Negatives

Work with a partner. Read each example below. Circle every negative word. Then cut out the boxes and sort each example. Finally, work together to write your own examples in the boxes at the bottom.

Informal	Formal

✂

Nobody never did nothing.	They didn't let nobody play.
I don't like no other team.	He doesn't want any pie.
They didn't let anybody play.	She won't ever come.
I don't like any other team.	Nobody ever did anything.
She won't never come.	He doesn't want no pie.

LINGUISTIC DIFFERENCES

ASSESSMENT

PREPARING THE TEST

- Make one copy of **Practice Reproducible GW12** for each child.
- Write the child's name and today's date at the top of the assessment.

ADMINISTERING THE TEST

- Administer the assessment to children individually or in groups. If necessary, read each item together with children.
- Remind children to circle each sentence that is in standard, or formal, English.
- Answers are shown below. Each item focuses on the skills taught in the lesson identified.

1. Answer: Circle around *Kim's dress is blue.* (Lesson 2)

2. Answer: Circle around *Jay has two dogs.* (Lesson 3)

3. Answer: Circle around *Yesterday I painted a picture.* (Lesson 4)

4. Answer: Circle around *That book is yellow.* (Lesson 5)

5. Answer: Circle around *He sings a song.* (Lesson 6)

6. Answer: Circle around *They were skating.* (Lesson 7)

7. Answer: Circle around *Al does a good job.* (Lesson 8)

8. Answer: Circle around *Whose coat is this?* (Lesson 9)

9. Answer: Circle around *She usually wears glasses.* (Lesson 10)

10. Answer: Circle around *Nobody ever did that.* (Lesson 11)

SCORING THE TEST

- Total the number of items answered correctly.
- Use the Percentage Table below to identify a percentage.
- Analyze each child's errors, using the lesson numbers provided above.
- Reteach those lessons for skills that caused the child difficulty.

Percentage Table			
10 correct	100%	**5 correct**	50%
9 correct	90%	**4 correct**	40%
8 correct	80%	**3 correct**	30%
7 correct	70%	**2 correct**	20%
6 correct	60%	**1 correct**	10%

Grammar Test

Read each pair of sentences. Circle the sentence that is written in formal, or standard, English.

1. Kim dress is blue.   Kim's dress is blue.

2. Jay has two dogs.   Jay has two dog.

3. Yesterday I painted a picture.   Yesterday I paint a picture.

4. That book be yellow.   That book is yellow.

5. He sings a song.   He sing a song.

6. They were skating.   They was skating.

7. Al do a good job.   Al does a good job.

8. Whose coat is this?   Who coat is this?

9. She be wearing glasses.   She usually wears glasses.

10. Nobody never did that.   Nobody ever did that.

<u>GRAMMAR</u>

Nouns for People and Animals

TEACH/MODEL

Introduce the Concept   Ground the discussion of grammar in concepts and distinctions that children make in their everyday lives. Keep the examples singular.

- Have a boy stand up. Say: *[Name] is a boy*. Write the word *boy* on the board. Have a girl stand up. Say: *[Name] is a girl*. Write the word *girl*. Write *brother, sister, father, mother*. Read each word. Explain that these are other names for people.

- Use pictures in books or magazines to find and name pictures of individual animals. Avoid proper names and plural nouns. Write each word on the board.

Explain Nouns for People and Animals   Tell children that each word on the board names a person or animal. Explain that these words are all called nouns. Say: *Different words can have different jobs in a sentence. The job of a noun is to name a person, place, animal, or thing.* Create a list like the one below. Sort the words on the board into two columns. Work with children to add more words.

People	Animals
boy	cow
girl	ape
sister	horse

PRACTICE/APPLY

Practice Reproducible   Copy and distribute **Practice Reproducible GW13**. Read the directions with children. Discuss each picture. Then have children complete the exercises. Provide corrective feedback.

English Learners

Common Nouns In languages such as Spanish and French, nouns are masculine or feminine. Point out that while some nouns in English refer to males or females (*boy, girl, uncle, aunt*), English nouns do not have masculine and feminine endings.

Linguistic Differences

African American Vernacular English (AAVE) AAVE is a language system with well-formed rules for sounds, grammar, and meanings. You will help speakers of AAVE by focusing on those places where AAVE differs from standard English and by teaching those patterns that will have the most immediate impact on students' reading and writing development. (See Linguistic Differences: Informal and Formal Patterns on pp. 2–3.)

© Macmillan/McGraw-Hill

Answer Key: Sample Answers: **1.** man **2.** cow **3.** *The <u>girl</u> tags the <u>boy</u>.* **4.** *The <u>dog</u> licks the <u>boy</u>.* **5.** *The <u>boy</u> throws to the <u>girl</u>.*

Nouns for People and Animals

Look at each picture. Write the noun that names it.

1.	_____
2. 	_____

Look at each picture. Add two nouns to finish each sentence.

3. 	The _____ tags the _____ .
4. 	The _____ licks the _____ .
5. 	The _____ throws to the _____ .

GRAMMAR

Nouns for Things

TEACH/MODEL

Introduce the Concept Ground the discussion of grammar in concepts and distinctions that children make in their everyday lives. Keep the examples singular.

- Hold up a book. Say: *This is a book.* Write the word *book* on the board.

- Point to other classroom objects, such as a table, a chair, a light. Name each thing, and write each word on the board. Explain that these are all words for things.

- Use pictures in books or magazines to find and name pictures of individual objects. Write each word on the board.

Explain Nouns for Things Read and discuss the words on the board. Tell children that each word names a thing. Explain that these words are all called nouns.

- Say: *Different words can have different jobs in a sentence. The job of a noun is to name a person, place, animal, or thing.*

- Create a list like the one shown below. Work with children to add more words.

Things	
apple	basket
fence	paper
skateboard	fountain
computer	calendar

PRACTICE/APPLY

Practice Reproducible Copy and distribute **Practice Reproducible GW14.** Read the directions with children. Discuss each picture. Then have children complete the exercises. Provide corrective feedback.

Answer Key: Sample Answers: **1.** net **2.** tub **3.** *A bat is near the hat.* **4.** *A book is on the couch.* **5.** *The roof is on the house.*

© Macmillan/McGraw-Hill

Nouns for Things

Look at each picture. Write the noun that names it.

1.

_____

2.

_____

Look at each picture. Add two nouns to finish each sentence.

3.

A _____ is near the _____ .

4.

A _____ is on the _____ .

5.

The _____ is on the _____ .

GRAMMAR

Nouns for Places

TEACH/MODEL

Introduce the Concept   Ground the discussion of grammar in concepts and distinctions that children make in their everyday lives. Keep the examples singular.

- Say: *We are in school.* Write the word *school* on the board. Say: *Each one of us lives at home.* Write the word *home* on the board.

- Write *town, city, state* on the board. Read each word with children. Explain that these are other names for places.

- Use pictures in books or magazines to find and name pictures of individual places. Avoid proper nouns and plural nouns. Write each word on the board.

Explain Nouns for Places   Read and discuss the words on the board. Tell children that each word names a place. Explain that these words are all called nouns.

- Say: *Different words can have different jobs in a sentence. The job of a noun is to name a person, place, animal, or thing.*

- Create a list like the one shown below. Work with children to add more words.

Places	
forest	office
park	library
airport	mall
restaurant	jungle

PRACTICE/APPLY

Practice Reproducible   Copy and distribute **Practice Reproducible GW15.** Read the directions with children. Discuss each picture. Then have children complete the exercises. Provide corrective feedback.

Answer Key: Sample Answers: **1.** yard **2.** zoo **3.** *She is in a* <u>store</u>. **4.** *They are at the* <u>beach</u>. **5.** *She works on a* <u>farm</u>.

Nouns for Places

Look at each picture. Write the noun that names it.

1. _____

2.  _____

Look at each picture. Add one noun to finish each sentence.

3. She is in a _____ .

4.  They are at the

_____ .

5. She works on a

_____ .

GRAMMAR

Action Verbs (Present)

TEACH/MODEL

Introduce the Concept   Ground the discussion of grammar in concepts and distinctions that children make in their everyday lives.

- Walk across the room. Say: *I walk.* Write the word *walk* on the board. Have a boy walk across the room. Say: *He walks.* Have a girl walk across the room. Say: *She walks.* Write the word *walks* on the board. Sit down. Say: *I sit.* Write the word *sit* on the board. Have the girl sit down. Say: *She sits.* Have the boy sit down. Say: *He sits.* Write the word *sits* on the board.

- Have children perform other simple actions, such as running, jumping, dancing. Write each word on the board, and read it with children.

Explain Action Verbs   Read and discuss the words on the board. Tell children that each word names an action. Explain that these words are called verbs.

- Say: *Different words can have different jobs in a sentence. The job of a verb is to tell what someone or something is or does. These verbs tell what someone does.*

- Create a list like the one below. Help children add words. Say: *The ending* -s *is added to many verbs, such as* shout, *to change* I shout *to* He shouts *or* She shouts.

Action Verbs	
shout	hop
read	look
grow	sing

PRACTICE/APPLY

Practice Reproducible   Copy and distribute **Practice Reproducible GW16.** Read the directions with children. Discuss each picture. Then have children complete the exercises. Provide corrective feedback.

English Learners

Present Tense Verbs English verb endings are simpler than verb endings in languages such as Spanish and Polish, which use different endings for person and number. However, children may need practice adding *-s* or *-es* to present tense verbs with third-person singular subjects.

Answer Key: 1. dig **2.** skate **3.** *The baby* sleeps. **4.** *A family* cooks. **5.** *The boy* reads.

Action Verbs (Present)

Look at each picture. Write a verb that names what is happening.

1. 	
2.	

Look at each picture. Add a verb to finish each sentence.

3. 	The baby _____ .
4. 	A family _____ .
5.	The boy _____ .

GRAMMAR

Irregular Verbs: *is*

TEACH/MODEL

Introduce the Concept   Ground the discussion of grammar in concepts and distinctions that children make in their everyday lives.

* Ask a girl to stand by the door. Say: *She is at the door.* Write the sentence on the board and underline the word *is*. Then point to a boy sitting at his desk. Say: *He is at a desk.* Write the sentence on the board and underline the word *is*.

* Ask a boy to stand up. Say: *He is standing.* Write the sentence and underline *is*. Point to a girl sitting. Say: *She is sitting.* Write the sentence and underline *is*.

Introduce Irregular Verb *is*   Read each sentence and point to the word *is*. Tell children that the word *is* is a verb. Say: *Different words have different jobs in a sentence. The job of a verb is to tell what someone or something is or does.*

* Reread the first sentence: *She is at the door.* Say: *In this sentence,* is *is the main verb. It tells where someone is.* Reread the second sentence: *He is standing.* Circle *is standing.* Say: *In this sentence,* is *is the helping verb. The verb* is *helps the word* standing *tell about an action that is happening now.*

* Create a chart like the one shown below. Sort the examples on the board into each column. Work with children to add more examples.

Main Verb *is*	Helping Verb *is*
She is at the door. He is at a desk.	He is standing. She is sitting.

PRACTICE/APPLY

Practice Reproducible   Copy and distribute **Practice Reproducible GW17**. Read the directions with children. Discuss each picture. Then have children complete the exercises. Provide corrective feedback.

English Learners

Learning Verb Forms Spanish, like English, has irregular verbs (such as *ser*, which means "to be," and *ir*, "to go"). Challenge children who are literate in Spanish to identify irregular Spanish verbs, and see whether English verbs with the same meanings are irregular.

Linguistic Differences

Including *is* and *are* To learn standard academic English, many speakers of AAVE will need to learn not to delete *is* and *are* when speaking and writing. For example, students might say *He my brother* or *She goin' over there.* (See Linguistic Differences: Verb *to be*, pp. 10–11.)

Answer Key: **1.** *The kite <u>is</u> in the sky.* **2.** *She <u>is</u> on the slide.* **3.** *The boy <u>is</u> the winner.* **4.** *The girl <u>is</u> singing.* **5.** *The man <u>is</u> chopping.*

Irregular Verbs: *is*

Look at each picture. Add the verb is to finish each sentence.

1.		The kite _____ in the sky.
2.		She _____ on the slide.
3.		The boy _____ the winner.
4.		The girl _____ singing.
5.		The man _____ chopping.

GRAMMAR

Identifying Subjects

TEACH/MODEL

Introduce the Concept   Say: *The job of a sentence is to tell people what they need to know.*

- Write: *reads.* Then ask: *Is this everything you need to know? What else do you need to know?* Guide children to explain that they need to know who reads.

- Have a child in the class say *My father reads.* Write: *My father reads.* Capitalize the first letter, add a period at the end, and circle *My father.* Read the sentence with children. Ask: *Is this a complete thought now?* Guide children to explain that you added the words for the person who does the action.

- Write: *listens.* Ask: *What else do we need to know?* Guide children to explain that they need to know who listens. Then write: *The class listens.* Capitalize the first letter, add a period, and circle *The class.* Then read and discuss the sentence.

- Write: *is here.* Repeat the routine. Then write: *He is here.* Circle *is.* Emphasize that you created a complete thought by naming who is here. Emphasize that a sentence always begins with a capital letter and ends with a punctuation mark. Point out that this is how you wrote each sentence.

Define Subjects   Say: *The words in a sentence have different jobs. The job of the subject is to tell who or what does the action.*

- Point to the words that you circled in the first sentence *(My father).* Say: *These words tell who does the action. They are the subject, or naming part, of this sentence.* Point to the word you circled in the last sentence *(he).* Say: *This word tells who is somewhere. It is the subject of this sentence.*

- Have children read other sentences on the board and identify each subject.

- Write the sentences below. Work together to read each sentence and identify the subject. Point out the capital letter at the beginning and the period at the end.

My sister rides her bike.	A teacher is in the hall.
The baby is in the crib.	A squirrel hides nuts.
The bell rings.	My dad bakes bread.

PRACTICE/APPLY

Practice Reproducible   Copy and distribute **Practice Reproducible GW18.** Read the directions with children. Discuss each picture. Then have children complete the exercises. Provide corrective feedback.

Answer Key: 1. *Dad* **2.** *A fish* **3.** *Peg* **4.** *The class* **5.** *He* **6.** *The clock* **7.** Sample Answer: *The girl plants a flower.* **8.** Sample Answer: *A duck quacks.* **9.** Sample Answer: *A chick comes out of the egg.*

Identifying Subjects

Read each sentence. Circle each subject.

1. Dad rakes the leaves.

2. A fish swims.

3. Peg sings a song.

4. The class takes a trip.

5. He meets my friend.

6. The clock ticks.

Look at each picture. Write a subject to finish each sentence. Use a capital letter.

7.	_____ plants a flower.
8.	_____ quacks.
9.	_____ comes out of the egg.

GRAMMAR

Identifying Predicates

TEACH/MODEL

Introduce the Concept   Say: *The job of a sentence is to tell people what they need to know.*

- Write: *My mother.* Then ask: *Is this everything you need to know? What else do you need to know?* Guide children to explain that they need to what the mother does.

- Then write: *My mother walks.* Capitalize the first letter, add a period at the end of the sentence, and circle the verb you added. Then read the sentence with children. Ask: *Is this a complete thought now?*

- Write: *The class.* Ask: *What else do we need to know?* Guide children to explain that they need to know what the class does. Then write: *The class hears the teacher.* Add a period, and circle *hears the teacher.* Then read and discuss the sentence.

- Write: *She.* Repeat the routine. Then write: *She is here.* Circle *is here.* Emphasize that you created a sentence by telling where *she* is. Emphasize that a sentence always begins with a capital letter and ends with a punctuation mark.

Define Predicates   Say: *The words in a sentence have different jobs. The job of the predicate is to tell what the subject, or naming part, is or does. It always includes a verb.*

- Point to the first verb that you circled *(walks).* Say: *This word tells the action. It is the predicate of this sentence.* Point to the last words you circled *(is here).* Say: *This tells where or what someone or something is. It is the predicate of this sentence.*

- Have children read the other sentences and identify each predicate.

- Write the following sentences on the board. Work together to read each sentence and identify each predicate. Point out the capital letter at the beginning of each sentence and the period at the end.

Bob plays.	He waits in line.
Grandma shops.	Lois drinks milk.
A bee flies.	Rain soaks the ground.

PRACTICE/APPLY

Practice Reproducible   Copy and distribute **Practice Reproducible GW19.** Read the directions with children. Discuss each picture. Then have children complete the exercises. Provide corrective feedback.

Answer Key: 1. *dances* **2.** *blows* **3.** *swims* **4.** *writes a story* **5.** *pack my bag* **6.** *makes her bed* **7.** Sample Answer: *The bear <u>sleeps</u>.* **8.** Sample Answers: *A boy <u>draws</u>* or *A boy <u>draws a picture</u>.* **9.** Sample Answers: *The cat <u>licks</u>* or *The cat <u>licks its paw</u>.*

Identifying Predicates

Read each sentence. Circle each predicate.

1. The child dances.
2. The wind blows.
3. A family swims.

4. Ted writes a story.
5. I pack my bag.
6. Kim makes her bed.

Look at each picture. Write a predicate to finish each sentence. Use a period.

7.		The bear
8.		A boy
9.		The cat

GRAMMAR

Complete Sentences

TEACH/MODEL

Introduce the Concept   Say: *The job of a sentence is to tell people what they need to know: a complete thought. A complete sentence tells a complete thought.*

- Write: *My friend.* Then ask: *Is this everything you need to know? What else do you need to know?* Guide children to say that they need to know what the friend does. Then write: *My friend rides the bus.* Read it aloud. Ask: *Is this a complete thought now?* Guide children to say that you added a verb to tell what the subject does.

- Write: *is in the yard.* Ask: *What else do we need to know?* Guide children to explain that they need to know what is in the yard. Then write: *A chicken is in the yard.* Ask: *Is this a complete thought now?* Guide children to explain that you added words to tell who or what does the action.

Define Complete Sentences   Say: *A complete sentence has two parts: a subject and a predicate. The subject, or naming part, tells who or what does the action. The predicate, or action part, tells what the subject is or does. It always includes a verb.*

- Reread the first sentence. Underline the subject *(My friend)* and circle the predicate *(rides the bus).* Then read the second sentence. Underline the subject *(A chicken)* and circle the predicate *(is in the yard).* Remind children that a sentence always begins with a capital letter and ends with a punctuation mark.

- Write the following sentences and read them aloud. Together, underline each subject and circle each predicate. Point out the capital letter and the period.

Angela sings.	We run to the car.
My sister climbs.	Snow covers the street.

PRACTICE/APPLY

Practice Reproducible   Copy and distribute **Practice Reproducible GW20.** Read the directions and have children complete the exercises. Provide feedback.

English Learners

Subjects and Predicates The typical English sequence of subject then predicate is not standard in some languages. For example, in Spanish the verb often appears before the subject, while in Korean and Hindi the verb typically appears at the end of a sentence.

Answer Key: 1. S: *Kate* P: *plays* **2.** S: *A boat* P: *sails* **3.** S: *The boy* P: *smiles* **4.** S: *We* P: *feed the birds* **5.** S: *She* P: *opens the box* **6.** S: *The turtle* P: *crawls* **7.** Sample Answer: *The artist paints.* **8.** Sample Answer: *A rocket flies.* **9.** Sample Answer: *The candle burns.*

Complete Sentences

Read each sentence. Underline each subject and circle each predicate.

1. Kate plays.

2. A boat sails.

3. The boy smiles.

4. We feed the birds.

5. She opens the box.

6. The turtle crawls.

Write three complete sentences. Choose a subject and a predicate from the box. Use a capital letter and a period.

Subjects	Predicates
The artist	burns
A rocket	paints
The candle	flies

7. _____

8. _____

9. _____

GRAMMAR

Fixing Sentence Fragments

TEACH/MODEL

Introduce the Concept Say: *The job of a sentence is to tell people what they need to know. A complete sentence tells a complete thought.* Review that a complete sentence has both a subject, or naming part, and a predicate, or action part.

• Write this sentence on the board: *Anton eats lunch.* Underline the subject *(Anton)* and circle the predicate *(eats lunch)*. Say: *This is a complete sentence.*

Introduce Sentence Fragments Tell children that if a sentence is not complete, it is called a sentence fragment. Explain that a sentence fragment is missing either the subject (naming part) or the predicate (action part).

• Write: *buys toys.* Explain that this is a fragment. Point out that the subject is missing. Say: *Do you know who buys toys? No, because there is no subject.*

• Write: *Now Juanita.* Explain that this is a fragment because the predicate is missing. Say: *Do you know what Juanita does? No, because there is no predicate.*

Model Fixing Fragments Tell children they can fix fragments by adding either a subject or a predicate. Fix the sentences you wrote above.

•Add *Angela* to write *Angela buys toys.* Tell children you added a subject to complete the sentence. Add *runs home* to write *Now Juanita runs home.* Tell children you added a predicate to complete the sentence.

• Model fixing these fragments by adding subjects: *paints a picture; climbs the stairs.* Model fixing these fragments by adding predicates: *The boy; My mom.*

PRACTICE/APPLY

Practice Reproducible Copy and distribute **Practice Reproducible GW21.** Read the directions. Have children complete the exercises. Provide feedback.

English Learners

Sentence Fragments Spanish- and Chinese-speaking children may omit some pronouns as sentence subjects because in their home languages the pronoun may be unnecessary. For example, the Spanish equivalent of *Am reading* is a complete sentence.

Linguistic Differences

Including *is* and *are* To learn standard academic English, many speakers of African American Vernacular English will need to learn not to delete *is* and *are* when speaking and writing. For example, students might say *He my brother* or *She goin' over there.* (See Linguistic Differences: Verb *to be*, pp. 10–11.)

Answer Key: 3., 4., 6.: Complete Sentences. **7.** Sample Answer: *A horse eats hay.* **8.** Sample Answer: *The dog barks.* **9.** Sample Answer: *A cow sleeps.* **10.** Sample answer: *The farmer drives a tractor.*

© Macmillan/McGraw-Hill

Fixing Sentence Fragments

Read each group of words. Circle each complete sentence.

1. Tall building.

2. A cookie and a cake.

3. The ball bounces.

4. Jenna climbs the tree.

5. Runs away.

6. The sun shines.

Fix each fragment. Add a subject or a predicate from the box. Rewrite it on the line that follows. Use a capital letter and a period.

Subjects	Predicates
the farmer	barks
a horse	sleeps

7. Eats hay. _____

8. The dog. _____

9. A cow. _____

10. Drives a tractor. _____

_____

Assessment

PREPARING THE TEST

- Copy **Practice Reproducible GW22.** Make one copy of the assessment for each child.
- Write the child's name and today's date at the top of the assessment.

ADMINISTERING THE TEST

- Administer the assessment to children individually or in groups.
- If necessary, read each item together with children.
- Answers are shown below. Each item focuses on the skills taught in the lesson or lessons identified.

  1. Answer: *mouse* (Lesson 13–Lesson 15)

  2. Answer: *town* (Lesson 13–Lesson 15)

  3. Answer: *draw* (Lesson 16)

  4. Answer: *is* (Lesson 17)

  5. Answer: *The baker* (Lesson 18)

  6. Answer: *sells clocks* (Lesson 19)

  7. Answer: *The man shovels snow.* (Lesson 20–21)

  8. Answer: *The monkey climbs a tree.* (Lesson 20–21)

SCORING THE TEST

- Total the number of items answered correctly.
- Use the Percentage Table below to identify a percentage.
- Analyze each child's errors, using the lesson numbers provided above.
- Reteach those lessons for skills that caused the child difficulty.

Percentage Table			
8 correct	100%	**3 correct**	38%
7 correct	88%	**2 correct**	25%
6 correct	75%	**1 correct**	13%
5 correct	63%	**0 correct**	0%
4 correct	50%		

Practice
Reproducible
GW22

Grammar Test

Complete each item.

1. Read each word. Circle the noun.

   swim   mouse   read

2. Read each word. Circle the noun.

   grab   sleep   town

3. Read each word. Circle the verb.

   draw   glass   queen

4. Read each word. Circle the verb.

   shell   is   sand

5. Read the sentence. Underline the subject.
   The baker makes a cake.

6. Read the sentence. Circle the predicate.
   The woman sells clocks.

Fix each fragment. Add a subject or a predicate from the box. Rewrite it on the line that follows. Use a capital letter and a period.

Subjects	Predicates
the monkey	shovels snow

7. The man _____

8. _____ climbs a tree.

<u>**GRAMMAR**</u>

Declarative Sentences

TEACH/MODEL

Introduce Declarative Sentences   Write *declarative* on the board, and have children say it with you. Say: *A declarative sentence is one kind of complete sentence. A declarative sentence, or statement, tells about someone or something.*

- Have a girl stand up. Say: *The girl stands*. Write the sentence. Say: *This is a declarative sentence because it tells about someone.* Then explain that a declarative sentence begins with a capital letter and ends with a period.

- Place a book on a desk. Say: *A book is on the desk*. Write the sentence. Say: *This is a declarative sentence because it tells about something. It tells about the book.* Point out the capital letter and the period.

Model Identifying Declarative Sentences   Reread these sentences. Review that the subject, or naming part, tells what someone is or does. Underline the subject in both sentences *(The girl; A book)*. Review that the predicate, or action part, tells what the subject is or does. Circle the predicate in both sentences *(stands; is on the desk)*. Point out that each declarative sentence is a complete sentence because it has both a subject and a predicate. Write: *walks her dog*. Review that this is a sentence fragment because it does not have a subject. Write: *My friend walks her dog.* Underline the subject *(My friend)* and circle the predicate *(walks her dog)*. Explain that this is a complete sentence because it has both a subject and a predicate. Point out the capital letter and the period. Emphasize that this is a declarative sentence because it tells about someone or something. Write: *The horse* and *The horse eats grass.* Repeat the routine.

PRACTICE/APPLY

Practice Reproducible   Distribute **Practice Reproducible GW23.** Read the directions and have children complete the exercises. Provide feedback.

English Learners
Forming Declarative Sentences
Children who have begun to read in Spanish and other alphabetic languages may recognize that sentences begin with capital letters and end with periods.

Answer Key: **1.** sentence fragment **2.** declarative sentence **3.** declarative sentence **4.** sentence fragment **5.** declarative sentence **6.** sentence fragment **7.** declarative sentence **8.** sentence fragment **9.** declarative sentence **10.** declarative sentence **11.** Sample Answer: My name is Maya. **12.** Sample Answer: I am seven years old.

Declarative Sentences

Read each group of words. Circle each declarative sentence. Underline each sentence fragment.

1. Can paint.
2. The cat is sleeping.
3. My name is Tran.
4. The truck.
5. Luc owns a bird.

6. Airplane in the sky.
7. My dad likes to run.
8. Maya likes.
9. I can see the moon tonight.
10. A cow drinks water.

Read each question. Then write a declarative sentence to answer it. Begin each statement with a capital letter. End it with a period.

11. What is your name? _____

12. How old are you? _____

GRAMMAR

Interrogative Sentences

TEACH/MODEL

Introduce Interrogative Sentences Write the word *interrogative* on the board, and have children say it with you. Say: *An interrogative sentence, or question, is another kind of complete sentence. An interrogative sentence asks a question.* Have a child stand. Say: *Who is standing?* Write the sentence. Say: *This is an interrogative sentence because it asks a question.* Explain that an interrogative sentence begins with a capital letter and ends with a question mark. Say: *Is the teacher talking?* Write the sentence. Say: *This is an interrogative sentence because it also asks a question.* Point out that it also begins with a capital letter and ends with a question mark. Review that the subject, or naming part, tells what someone is or does. Underline both subjects *(Who; The teacher)*. Review that the predicate, or action part, tells what the subject is or does. Circle both predicates. *(is standing; is and talking)*. Point out that each interrogative sentence is complete because it has both a subject and a predicate.

Model Identifying Interrogative Sentences Answer each interrogative sentence that you wrote. Point to: *Who is standing?* Then answer, using the name of the child standing: *[Name] is standing.* Write this near the interrogative sentence, and have the child sit down. Say: *This is a declarative sentence because it tells about someone or something. It answers a question.* Identify the subject (*[name]*) and predicate (*is standing*). Point out that both sentences begin with a capital letter, while the declarative sentence ends with a period and the interrogative sentence ends with a question mark. Point to: *Is the teacher talking?* Then answer: *The teacher is talking.* Write this sentence, and repeat the routine. Point out that both sentences have the same words but in a different order.

PRACTICE/APPLY

Practice Reproducible Distribute **Practice Reproducible GW24.** Read the directions and have children complete the exercises. Provide feedback.

English Learners
Forming Interrogative Sentences
Speakers of Asian languages often form interrogatives by adding words to declarative sentences, comparable to *The food is hot, no?* or *You see or not see the bird?* Provide English models.

Answer Key: 1. interrogative **2.** declarative **3.** declarative **4.** interrogative **5.** interrogative **6.** interrogative **7.** declarative **8.** interrogative **9.** interrogative **10.** declarative **11.** Sample Answer: What is in the box? **12.** Sample Answer: Do you want to play a game?

Interrogative Sentences

Read each sentence. Circle each declarative sentence. Underline each interrogative sentence.

1. Is Reggie sleeping?

2. Reggie is sleeping.

3. A wolf is an animal.

4. Is it time to play?

5. Will you read me a story?

6. Is Kayla reading?

7. Kayla is reading.

8. When can I go out?

9. Can you bake a cake?

10. Bill can jump.

Write two interrogative sentences. Begin each with a capital letter. End each with a question mark.

11. Suppose you saw a friend with a big box.
Write a question you might ask about the box.

_____

_____

12. Suppose you want to play a game at recess.
Write a question you would ask a friend.

_____

_____

GRAMMAR

Declarative and Interrogative Sentences

TEACH/MODEL

Review Declarative and Interrogative Sentences Say: *A declarative sentence is one kind of complete sentence. It tells about someone or something. An interrogative sentence is another kind of complete sentence. An interrogative sentence asks a question. Each has a subject, or naming part, and a predicate, or action part.*

- Write: *What can jump?* Review that this is an interrogative sentence because it asks a question. Then write: *Monkeys can jump.* Review that this is a declarative sentence because it tells about someone or something.

- Underline the subject in each sentences *(What; Monkeys)*. Circle the predicate in both sentences. *(can jump; can jump).* Point out that both sentences begin with a capital letter, while the declarative sentence ends with a period and the interrogative sentence ends with a question mark.

- Write: *Can cats jump?* Review that this is also an interrogative sentence. Then write: *Cats can jump.* Review that this is a declarative sentence. Discuss capitalization and punctuation. Underline the subject in each sentence *(cats; Cats).* Circle the predicate in each sentence *(can* and *jump; can jump).* Then point out that both sentences have the same words but each puts them in a different order.

Model Identifying Declarative and Interrogative Sentences Write the following sentences on the board. Read each sentence. Work together with children to identify which sentences are declarative and which are interrogative. Point out the capital letter at the beginning of each sentence and the period or question mark at the end.

I eat lunch.	They played tag.
Is the dog sleeping?	Who played tag?
The dog is sleeping.	Is it time for gym?

PRACTICE/APPLY

Practice Reproducible Distribute **Practice Reproducible GW25.** Read the directions and have children complete the exercises. Provide feedback.

Answer Key: 1. declarative **2.** interrogative **3.** interrogative **4.** declarative **5.** interrogative **6.** declarative **7.** declarative **8.** interrogative **9.** declarative **10.** interrogative **11.** Sample Answer: The name of my school is [Name]. **12.** Sample Answer: When can I eat again?

Declarative and Interrogative Sentences

Read each sentence. Circle each declarative sentence. Underline each interrogative sentence.

1. My fish likes to swim.
2. May I pat your dog?
3. Can a cat bark?
4. Kim likes to dance.
5. Where is Jamil?

6. My bird is in the cage.
7. Tina rides a bike.
8. Will Peng eat lunch with us?
9. Eva is going home on the bus.
10. Who can climb the tree?

Write two sentences. Remember to begin each sentence with a capital letter. Use the correct punctuation.

11. What is the name of your school?
    Write one declarative sentence.

    _____

    _____

12. Suppose a cat could talk. What question would it ask? Write one interrogative sentence.

    _____

    _____

GRAMMAR

Exclamatory Sentences

TEACH/MODEL

Introduce Exclamatory Sentences Write the word *exclamatory* on the board, and have children say it with you. Say: *An exclamatory sentence is another kind of complete sentence. An exclamatory sentence shows strong feeling or emotion. It begins with a capital letter and ends with an exclamation point.*

- Ask a child to say this sentence as if he or she were bored: *I like recess.* Write this sentence on the board. Point out the capital letter and the period.

- Ask the child to say this sentence in an excited way: *I like recess!* Point out the capital letter and the exclamation point. Say: *This is an exclamatory sentence. The exclamation point shows that a sentence should be read with strong feeling.*

- Write this sentence frame on the board: *I like _____ !* Have children complete the sentence with examples of animals, people, or objects. Write their sentences on the board. For example: *I like ice cream!*

- Review that the subject, or naming part, tells what someone is or does. Underline the subject in each exclamatory sentence *(I).* Review that the predicate, or action part, tells what the subject is or does. Circle the predicate in each sentence *(like recess; like ice cream,* etc.*).* Point out that each exclamatory sentence is a complete sentence because it has both a subject and a predicate.

Model Identifying Exclamatory Sentences Write the following pairs of sentences on the board. Work together with children to identify which sentences are exclamatory and which are declarative. Point out the capital letter at the beginning of each sentence and the period or exclamation point at the end. Have children show strong feeling when they read each exclamatory sentence.

We can see the sun.	We can see the sun!
They played tag!	They played tag.

Practice Reproducible Distribute **Practice Reproducible GW26.** Read the directions and have children complete the exercises. Provide feedback.

English Learners

Forming Exclamatory Sentences
English learners may need to practice correct word order in exclamatory sentences. Have children make sentence strips, correcting exclamations like *We enjoy very much movies!*

Answer Key: 1. exclamatory **2.** exclamatory **3.** declarative **4.** exclamatory **5.** declarative **6.** declarative **7.** exclamatory **8.** exclamatory **9.** declarative **10.** declarative **11.** Sample answer: I love to skate! **12.** Sample answer: I love enchiladas!

Exclamatory Sentences

Read each sentence. Circle each exclamatory sentence. Underline each declarative sentence.

1. I can see the moon! **6.** She picks a flower.

2. You are very funny! **7.** He is fast!

3. I can see the book. **8.** I want an apple!

4. I like your doll! **9.** She wants an airplane.

5. I like the truck. **10.** He wants to run.

Write two exclamatory sentences. Remember to begin each sentence with a capital letter. Use the correct punctuation.

11. What is one thing you love to do? _____

_____

12. What is your favorite food? _____

_____

GRAMMAR

Identifying Kinds of Sentences

TEACH/MODEL

Review Declarative, Interrogative, and Exclamatory Sentences Say:
*Declarative sentences, interrogative sentences, and exclamatory sentences are three
kinds of complete sentences. Each kind of sentence has a subject, or naming part,
and a predicate, or action part.*

- Write: *What is for lunch?* Review that this is an interrogative sentence because
  it asks a question. Point out the capital letter at the beginning of the sentence
  and the question mark at the end. Circle the subject *(What)* and underline the
  predicate *(is for lunch).*

- Write: *We are having pizza.* Review that this is a declarative sentence because
  it tells about someone or something. Point out the capital letter at the beginning of the sentence and the period at the end. Circle the subject *(We)* and
  underline the predicate *(are having pizza).*

- Write: *We are having pizza!* Review that this is an exclamatory sentence
  because it shows strong feeling. Point out the capital letter at the beginning of
  the sentence and the exclamation mark at the end. Circle the subject *(We)* and
  underline the predicate *(are having pizza).*

- Write: *Will you have dessert?* Then write: *You will have dessert.* Point out that
  both sentences have the same words but in a different order. Circle the subject
  in each sentence *(You)* and underline the predicate *(will have dessert).*

Model Identifying Kinds of Sentences Write these sentences on the board.
Work with children to identify which sentences are exclamatory, declarative,
and interrogative. Point out the capital letter at the beginning and the period,
question mark, or exclamation point at the end. Have children show strong
feeling when they read each exclamatory sentence.

Who is at the door?	My dad is at the door.
The letter is for me!	Is the letter for me?
It is raining today.	It is raining today!

PRACTICE/APPLY

Practice Reproducible Distribute **Practice Reproducible GW27.** Read the
directions and have children complete the exercises. Provide feedback.

Answer Key: **1.** exclamatory **2.** interrogative **3.** declarative **4.** exclamatory
5. declarative **6.** declarative **7.** interrogative **8.** exclamatory **9.** interrogative
10. Sample answer: I walk to school. **11.** Answers will vary. Sample answer: I can
fly! **12.** Sample answer: Can I please have a cheese sandwich?

Identifying Kinds of Sentences

Read each sentence. Circle each declarative sentence. Underline each interrogative sentence. Put a box around each exclamatory sentence.

1. You can win!

2. Is Carlos here?

3. Carlos is at home.

4. I love ice cream!

5. Mark can kick the ball.

6. My dad is working.

7. Can Mary help me?

8. My sister can read!

9. Where is my watch?

Write three sentences. Remember to begin each sentence with a capital letter. Use the correct end mark.

10. Do you walk to school? Write one declarative sentence. _____

    _____

11. What would you say if you could fly? Write one exclamatory sentence. _____

    _____

12. How would you ask someone to make your favorite sandwich? _____

    _____

GRAMMAR

Identifying Imperatives

TEACH/MODEL

Introduce Imperative Sentences   Write the word *imperative* on the board, and have children say it with you. Say: *An imperative sentence is another kind of complete sentence. An imperative sentence tells someone to do something. It begins with a capital letter and ends with a period.* Point at a child. Say: *Stand up.* Write this sentence. Say: *This is an imperative sentence. It tells someone to do something.* Point out the capital letter and the period. Point to the child standing. Say: *[Name] stands up.* Write this sentence. Say: *This is a declarative sentence. It tells about someone or something.* Point out the capital letter and the period. Repeat with other sentences. Point at another child, and say: *Close the door.* Then say: *[Name] closes the door.* Write both sentences. Repeat with other simple actions.

Discuss Subjects and Predicates   Review that the predicate, or action part, tells what someone is or does. Circle the predicate in each sentence you wrote *(Stand up; stands up; Close the door; closes the door)*. Review that the subject, or naming part, tells what someone is or does. Underline the subject in each declarative sentence *([Name])*. Point out that you didn't circle a subject in the imperative sentences. Say: *The subject of this imperative sentence is the person I was talking to. The subject is understood.* Model this concept by issuing other commands to children, such as *Sit down. Open the door.* Write these imperatives on the board.

Model Identifying Imperative Sentences   Write the following sentences on the board. Work together with children to identify which sentences are imperative and which are declarative. Point out capital letters and periods.

Drink water.   Dara drinks water.
Do your homework.   She does her homework.

PRACTICE/APPLY

Practice Reproducible   Distribute **Practice Reproducible GW28.** Read the directions and have children complete the exercises. Provide feedback.

> ### English Learners
> **Forming Imperative Sentences**
> Vietnamese speakers may recognize commands that include an adverb or another clue word: *Go to school now. Take this to the office; go now.*

Answer Key: 1. declarative **2.** imperative **3.** imperative **4.** declarative **5.** imperative **6.** declarative **7.** imperative **8.** imperative **9.** declarative **10.** imperative **11.** Sample Answer: Take turns. **12.** Sample Answer: Don't push.

© Macmillan/McGraw-Hill

Identifying Imperatives

Read each sentence. Circle each declarative sentence. Underline each imperative sentence.

1. Sara cleans her room.
2. Feed the fish.
3. Clean your room.
4. Zoe kicks the ball.
5. Kick the ball.
6. Kalil turns off the light.
7. Drink your milk.
8. Turn off the light.
9. Lia crosses the street.
10. Look before you cross the street.

On the lines below, write two school rules that you follow. Write each rule as an imperative sentence. Begin each imperative with a capital letter. End it with a period.

11. One school rule: _____

_____

12. Another school rule: _____

_____

GRAMMAR

Identifying Kinds of Sentences

TEACH/MODEL

Review Kinds of Sentences   Say: *Declarative, interrogative, exclamatory, and interrogative sentences are four kinds of complete sentences. Each kind of sentence has a subject, or naming part, and a predicate, or action part.*

- Write: *Who looks out the window?* Review that this is an interrogative sentence because it asks a question. Point out the capital letter and the question mark. Circle the subject *(Who)* and underline the predicate *(looks out the window).*

- Write: *Look out the window.* Review that this is an imperative sentence because it tells someone what to do. Point out the capital letter and the period. Underline the predicate *(Look out the window).* Explain that the subject is understood (you or the name of whoever you are talking to).

- Write: *She looks out the window.* Review that this is a declarative sentence because it tells about someone or something. Point out the capital letter at the beginning of the sentence and the period at the end. Circle the subject *(She)* and underline the predicate *(looks out the window).*

- Write: *I love looking out the window!* Review that this is an exclamatory sentence because it shows strong feeling. Point out the capital letter at the beginning of the sentence and the exclamation point at the end. Circle the subject *(I)* and underline the predicate *(love looking out the window).*

- Write: *Can I look out the window?* Then write: *I can look out the window.* Point out that each sentence has the same words but puts them in a different order. Circle both subjects *(I)* and underline the predicate *(can look out the window).*

Model Identifying Kinds of Sentences   Write the following sentences on the board. Work together with children to identify which sentences are exclamatory, which are declarative, which are interrogative, and which are imperative. Point out the capital letter and the period, question mark, or exclamation point.

She writes her name.	Write your name.
Who can draw?	They can draw.
Focus on your work.	Are you focusing on your work?

PRACTICE/APPLY

Practice Reproducible   Distribute **Practice Reproducible GW29.** Read the directions and have children complete the exercises. Provide feedback.

Answer Key: 1. exclamatory **2.** declarative **3.** declarative **4.** exclamatory **5.** imperative **6.** imperative **7.** interrogative **8.** interrogative **9–10.** Sentences will vary. Children should use the correct punctuation.

Identifying Kinds of Sentences

Read each sentence. Circle each declarative sentence. Underline each exclamatory sentence.

1. I like your dress!   3. Shayna likes to swing.

2. Ryan can play a game.   4. The sky is dark!

Read each sentence. Circle each imperative sentence. Underline each interrogative sentence.

5. Buckle your seat belt.   7. Can Juan help me?

6. Put away your game.   8. Is Tam on the slide?

Write two different kinds of sentences. Use a capital letter and the correct end mark.

11. _____

_____

12. _____

_____

GRAMMAR

Assessment

PREPARING THE TEST

- Make one copy of **Practice Reproducible GW30** for each child.
- Write the child's name and today's date at the top of the assessment.

ADMINISTERING THE TEST

- Administer the assessment to children individually or in groups.
- If necessary, read each item together with children.
- Answers are shown below. Each item focuses on the skills taught in the lesson identified.

  1. Answer: declarative sentence (Lesson 23)
  2. Answer: interrogative sentence (Lesson 24)
  3. Answer: interrogative sentence (Lesson 25)
  4. Answer: declarative sentence (Lesson 25)
  5. Answer: exclamatory sentence (Lesson 26)
  6. Answer: imperative sentence (Lesson 28)
  7. Answer: imperative sentence (Lesson 28)
  8. Answer: exclamatory sentence (Lesson 29)

SCORING THE TEST

- Total the number of items answered correctly.
- Use the Percentage Table below to identify a percentage.
- Analyze each child's errors, using the lesson numbers provided above.
- Reteach those lessons for skills that caused the child difficulty.

Percentage Table			
8 correct	100%	**3 correct**	38%
7 correct	88%	**2 correct**	25%
6 correct	75%	**1 correct**	13%
5 correct	63%	**0 correct**	0%
4 correct	50%		

Grammar Test

Read each sentence. Circle each declarative sentence. Underline each interrogative sentence.

1. Tonya rides the bus.

2. Does David ride his bike?

3. When can we play?

4. I like sledding.

Read each sentence. Circle each imperative sentence. Underline each interrogative sentence.

5. This flower is for you!

6. Mix an egg with some milk.

7. Make a sandwich.

8. I love my mom!

GRAMMAR

Singular and Plural Nouns

TEACH/MODEL

Introduce the Concept Ground the discussion of grammar in concepts and distinctions that children make in their everyday lives.

- Hand a child a book. Say: *[Name] has a book.* Write *book*. Then hand the child another book. Say: *[Name] has books.* Write *books*, underlining the *s*.

- Write *hat, dog, boy,* and *store* on the board. Explain that each of these words names one of something. Then write the words again, adding an *s* to make *hats, dogs, boys,* and *stores*. Explain that now each word means more than one.

- Have children name objects in the classroom that there are only one of and objects that there are more than one of. Write each word on the board.

Introduce Singular and Plural Nouns Read and discuss the words on the board. Tell children that these words are nouns because they name a person, animal, place, or thing. Say: *If a word tells about just one person, animal, place, or thing, that word is called a* **singular noun.** *If it tells about more than one, the word is called a* **plural noun.** *You add -s to a noun that means one to make it mean more than one.* Create a chart like the one shown. Underline the *-s*. Add more words.

Singular Nouns	Plural Nouns
hat	hats
dog	dogs
boy	boys
store	stores

PRACTICE/APPLY

Practice Reproducible Distribute **Practice Reproducible GW31.** Read the directions and have children complete the exercises. Provide feedback.

English Learners

Plural Nouns Spanish speakers use *-s* and *-es* endings for nouns. In some languages, including Chinese, Hmong, and Vietnamese, nouns do not have plural forms. Instead, the plural is indicated with an adjective.

Linguistic Differences

Plurals Most African American Vernacular English correctly uses plurals except when it involves "nouns of measure," as in *It cost five dollars* or *She owe me five dollars.* However, the plural /s/ is often absent in writing, and students will need additional instruction and practice. (See Linguistic Differences: Plural Patterns on pp. 6–7.)

Answer Key: **1.** trees **2.** sisters **3.** chicks **4.** pencils **5.** ponds **6.** *kites* **7.** *pigs* **8.** Ducks **9.** *blocks* **10.** Sentences will vary but each should use a plural noun with *-s.*

Singular and Plural Nouns

Write each singular noun so it is a plural noun.

1. tree _____   **4.** pencil _____

2. sister _____   **5.** pond _____

3. chick _____

Rewrite each sentence, using the plural noun in ( ).

6. I see (kite, kites) in the sky.

_____

7. The (pig, pigs) roll in the mud.

_____

8. (Ducks, Duck) swim in the pond.

_____

9. Sam plays with (blocks, block).

_____

Choose one of the plural nouns you wrote above. Write a sentence using this noun.

10. _____

_____

<u>**GRAMMAR**</u>

Plural Nouns with -es

TEACH/MODEL

Introduce the Concept Ground the discussion of grammar in concepts and distinctions that children make in their everyday lives.

- Give a brush to a child. Say: *[Name] has a brush.* Write the word *brush* on the board. Give the same child another brush. Say: *[Name] now has two brushes.* Write the word *brushes* on the board, underlining the *-es*.

- Follow this routine with these objects: a box, two boxes; a watch, two watches; and a glass, two glasses. Write each word on the board, underlining *-es*.

Introduce Plural Nouns with -es Read and discuss the words. Tell children that each word names one or more things. These words are called nouns. Review that one of something is singular and more than one is plural. Read the singular nouns on the board. Say: *To make most nouns mean more than one, you just add* -s. *But if nouns end with the letters* s, x, ch, *and* sh, *as in* glass, box, watch, and brush, *you add* -es *to make the noun mean more than one.* Create a chart like this one. Underline each *-es*. Work with children to add more words.

Singular Nouns	Plural Nouns
glass	glasses
box	boxes
watch	watches
brush	brushes

PRACTICE/APPLY

Practice Reproducible Distribute **Practice Reproducible GW32.** Read the directions and have children complete the exercises. Provide feedback.

English Learners

Irregular Plurals English learners might add *-s* to irregular nouns in sentences or to nouns for which English uses the singular for a quantity: *sheeps, mens, clothings.*

Answer Key: 1. boxes **2.** buses **3.** classes **4.** wishes **5.** benches **6.** dresses **7.** *beaches* **8.** *buses* **9.** *dishes* **10.** Sentences will vary but each should have a plural noun ending in *-es*.

© Macmillan/McGraw-Hill

Plural Nouns with -es

Write each singular noun so it is a plural noun.

1. box _____   4. wish _____

2. bus _____   5. bench _____

3. class _____   6. dress _____

**Circle the noun that best completes each
sentence. Then write the sentence correctly.**

7. Ted likes to swim at two (beach, beaches).

_____

8. Dad rides on three (bus, buses).

_____

9. Mom puts four (dish, dishes) on the table.

_____

**Choose one of the plural nouns you wrote above.
Write a sentence using this noun.**

10. _____

_____

_____

GRAMMAR

Plural Nouns: Spelling Changes

TEACH/MODEL

Introduce the Concept   Ground the discussion of grammar in concepts and distinctions that children make in their everyday lives.

• Find or draw pictures of the following: a child and children, a woman and women, a man and men, a baby and babies, a bunny and bunnies.

• Give one child the picture of a child and another the picture of children. Point to each picture and say: *This is a child. These are children.* Write the words *child* and *children* in two columns on the board.

• Repeat with the other singular-plural noun pairs. Write each word. Sort words into a chart like the one shown below.

Singular Nouns	Plural Nouns
child	children
woman	women
man	men
baby	babies
bunny	bunnies

Introduce Plural Nouns with Spelling Changes   Read and discuss the words in the chart. Tell children that some singular nouns change their spelling to become plural. Point to the singular nouns *child, woman,* and *man*. Explain that an *-s* is not added to make these nouns mean more than one. Have them read the plural for each singular noun: *children, women, men*. Point to the singular nouns *baby* and *bunny*. Explain that these nouns end with *-y*, so to make them plural, the *-y* is changed to *-i* and *-es* is added. Have them read the plurals for *baby* and *bunny*: *babies, bunnies*. Write other singular nouns ending in *-y*: *body, city, party, story*. Then write the plural for each noun. Read each noun with children.

PRACTICE/APPLY

Practice Reproducible   Distribute **Practice Reproducible GW33.** Read the directions and have children complete the exercises. Provide feedback.

Answer Key: 1. men 2. children 3. bodies 4. cities 5. parties 6. women 7. *children* 8. *bunnies* 9. *pennies* 10. Sentences will vary but each should include a plural noun with a spelling change.

Plural Nouns: Spelling Changes

Write each singular noun so it is a plural noun.

1. man _____   **4.** city _____

2. child _____   **5.** party _____

3. body _____   **6.** woman _____

Circle the noun that best completes each sentence. Then write the sentence correctly.

7. Three (child, children) play with a puppy.

_____

8. Many (bunny, bunnies) hop in the grass.

_____

9. Rob has hundreds of (penny, pennies) in a jar.

_____

Choose one of the plural nouns you wrote above. Write a sentence using this noun.

10. _____

<u>**GRAMMAR**</u>

Subject-Verb Agreement

TEACH/MODEL

Introduce the Concept   Ground the discussion of grammar in concepts and distinctions that children make in their everyday lives.

- Have a child demonstrate how to skip. Say: *A child skips.* Then write this sentence on the board. Read it with children.
- Have another child join the first and have both skip. Say: *The children skip.* Then write this sentence on the board. Read it with children.
- Follow this routine with these verbs: *claps, clap; walks, walk;* and *smiles, smile.* Continue to use *child* and *children* for the subjects.
- Circle the verbs. Remind children that verbs are action words that tell what someone does. Underline *child* and *children.* Remind children that each word is the subject of its sentence.

Introduce Subject-Verb Agreement   Read each sentence on the board. Point out that the verb changes depending on whether the subject is singular *(child)* or plural *(children).* Say: *When a verb tells about a noun that is singular or names one, add* -s *to the verb. For example, we say* Tim runs *not* Tim run. *When a verb tells about a noun that is plural, or names more than one, do not add* -s *to the verb. For example, we say* Cars honk *not* Cars honks. Sort verbs into a chart.

A child . . .	The children . . .
skips	skip
claps	clap
walks	walk

PRACTICE/APPLY

Practice Reproducible   Distribute **Practice Reproducible GW34.** Read the directions and have children complete the exercises. Provide feedback.

English Learners

Subject-Verb Agreement English learners might add -s to both the noun and the verb in a sentence: *The robots walks.* Reinforce that in English, -s is added for verbs with singular nouns *(A robot walks),* not for verbs with plural nouns *(The robots walk).*

Linguistic Differences

Subject-Verb Agreement To acquire standard academic English, AAVE speakers need to learn to use -s with a verb and the third person, as in *he is* and *he goes.* Many AAVE speakers will leave out the -s or place it elsewhere, as in *he go* or *we goes.* (See Linguistic Differences: Subject-Verb Agreement, pp. 12–13.)

Answer Key: 1. *eat* **2.** *stop* **3.** *reads* **4.** *plants* **5.** *clock* **6.** *stars* **7.** *frogs* **8.** Sentences will vary but each subject and verb must agree.

Subject-Verb Agreement

**Read each sentence. Circle the correct verb.
Then write the sentence on the line.**

1. Cows (eat, eats) grass.

_____

2. Buses (stop, stops) at the park.

_____

3. Jim (read, reads) a book.

_____

4. Amy (plant, plants) seeds.

_____

Read each sentence. Circle the correct noun.

5. One big (clock, clocks) ticks.

6. Many (star, stars) shine at night.

7. Six (frog, frogs) jump into the pond.

**Choose one of the plural nouns you circled
above. Write a sentence using this noun.**

8. _____

_____

<u>GRAMMAR</u>

Subject-Verb Agreement: *is*, *are*

TEACH/MODEL

Introduce the Concept   Ground the discussion of grammar in concepts and distinctions that children make in their everyday lives.

- Point to a book on a child's desk. Say: *The book is on the desk.* Then write this sentence. Read it with children. Put two books on another child's desk. Say: *The books are on the desk.* Then write this sentence on the board. Read it with children. Say: *We used* is *and* are *to tell where the book or books can be found.*

- Then ask a child to turn around several times. Say: *A child is turning.* Write this sentence. Have two children turn around. Say: *The children are turning.* Write this sentence. Say: *We used* is *and* are *to tell what the child or children are doing.*

- Circle the verbs. Remind children that verbs are action words that tell what someone or something is or does. Underline *book, books* and *child, children.* Remind children that each word is the subject of its sentence.

Introduce Subject-Verb Agreement with *is* and *are*   Read and discuss each sentence on the board. Point out that the verb changes depending on whether the subject is singular *(child, book)* or plural *(children, books).*

- Say: *When the subject is singular, these sentences use* is. *When the subject is plural, these sentences use* are.

- Write these examples: *Dolls are on the shelf. A toy truck is on the shelf.* Have children name the subject of each sentence and tell if it is singular or plural.

- Write these examples: *Planes are landing. A train is slowing down.* Have them name the subject of each sentence and tell if it is singular or plural.

PRACTICE/APPLY

Practice Reproducible   Distribute **Practice Reproducible GW35.** Read the directions and have children complete the exercises. Provide feedback.

English Learners

Learning Verb Forms Spanish, like English, has irregular verbs (such as *ser,* which means "to be," and *ir,* "to go"). Challenge students who are literate in Spanish to identify irregular Spanish verbs, and see whether English verbs with the same meanings are irregular.

Linguistic Differences

Including *is* and *are* To learn standard academic English, many AAVE speakers will need to learn not to delete *is* and *are* when speaking and writing. For example, students might say *He my brother* or *She goin' over there.* (See Linguistic Differences: Verb *to be,* pp. 10–11.)

Answer Key: 1. *is* **2.** *is* **3.** *are* **4.** *are* **5.** *is* **6.** *are* **7–8.** Sentences may vary but one should correctly use *is* and one should correctly use *are*.

Subject-Verb Agreement: *is*, *are*

**Circle the verb that best completes each
sentence. Then write the sentence correctly.**

1. Her party (is, are) on Friday.

_____

2. Mom (is, are) baking a cake.

_____

3. Friends (is, are) bringing gifts for Kay.

_____

4. Balloons (is, are) on the floor.

_____

5. Kay (is, are) having fun.

_____

6. The boys (is, are) jumping up and down.

_____

**Write two sentences. Use the verb *is* in one
sentence. Use the word *are* in the other sentence.**

7. _____

_____

8. _____

_____

Singular Pronouns: *I* and *me*

TEACH/MODEL

Introduce the Concept   Ground the discussion of grammar in concepts and distinctions that children make in their everyday lives.

- Point to yourself. Explain that when you talk about yourself, you can use your name or the word *I*. Say and demonstrate: *[Your own name] claps* and *I clap.* Write both of these sentences on the board. Read them with children.

- Explain that when you talk about yourself, you can also use your name or the word *me*. Say: *You talk to [your own name]. You talk to me.* Write both of these sentences on the board. Read them with children.

- Then have one child come stand with you in front of the class. Say: *[Child's name] and [your own name] stand* and *[Child's name] and I stand.* Write both sentences on the board. Discuss word order. Point out that the child's name is written first and *I* is written last.

Introduce Singular Pronouns *I* and *me*   Reread the sentences on the board. Circle *I* and *me*. Underline the nouns they replace. Explain that *I* and *me* are pronouns. Say: *The job of a pronoun is to stand for another word or words in a sentence. A pronoun stands for other words about people, places, or things.*

- Point out that the pronoun *I* is used in the subject, or naming part, of a sentence. Point out that the pronoun *me* is used in the predicate, or action part, of the sentence.

- Tell children that when they write *I* they should always use a capital letter.

- Write these examples on the board and discuss them. *I play a game. Mom and I clean. Dad gives me a book.*

Introduce Subject-Verb Agreement   Explain that if *I* is used alone in the subject, the verb that follows it does not add *-s*. Write: *I hop. I hops.* Ask: *Which is correct? (I hop.)* Cross out *I hops.* Provide other examples. Write: *[Child's name] and I hop. [Child's name] and I hops.* Ask: *Which is correct? ([Child's name] and I hop.)* Cross out *[Child's name] and I hops.* Provide other examples.

PRACTICE/APPLY

Practice Reproducible   Distribute **Practice Reproducible GW36.** Read the directions and have children complete the exercises. Provide feedback.

Answer Key: 1. *me* **2.** *I* **3.** *I* **4.** *I* **5.** *swim* **6.** *run* **7.** Sample Answer: read books **8.** Sample Answer: an apple

Singular Pronouns: *I* and *me*

Circle the pronoun that best completes each sentence. Then write the sentence correctly.

1. Sam and Clara talked to (I, me).

_____

2. (I, me) play a game.

_____

3. Dan and (I, me) washed the car.

_____

4. My sister and (I, me) go to West School.

_____

Circle the verb that best completes each sentence. Then write the sentence correctly.

5. I (swims, swim) in the pool each day.

_____

6. Carl and I (runs, run) races.

_____

Circle the pronoun in each sentence. Then complete each sentence with your own words.

7. A friend and I _____.

8. A friend gives me _____.

GRAMMAR

Singular Pronouns: *he/him, she/her, you,* and *it*

TEACH/MODEL

Introduce the Concept   Ground the discussion of grammar in concepts and distinctions that children make in their everyday life.

- Point to a boy in the group. Say: *When we talk about a boy, we can use his name or the word* he. Say: *[Name] sits* and *He sits*. Write and read these sentences.

- Point to a girl in the group. Say: *When we talk about a girl, we can use her name or the word* she. Say: *[Name] sits* and *She sits*. Write and read these sentences.

- Then say: *When we talk about someone else, we can also use the word* you. Point to the boy or the girl and say: *You sit*. Write and read this sentence.

- Now hand the boy a book. Say: *I give a book to [name]* and *I give it to him.* Repeat with the girl and the pronoun *her*. Write and read these sentences.

Introduce Singular Pronouns   Reread the sentences. Circle *he, him, she, her, you,* and *it*. Underline the nouns they replace. Explain that *he, him, she, her, you,* and *it* are pronouns. Explain that the job of a pronoun is to stand for other words. Explain that each is a singular pronoun that refers to only one person or thing. Explain that *he* and *she* are used only in the subject, or naming part, of a sentence. Point out that *him* and *her* are used in the predicate, or action part.

Introduce Subject-Verb Agreement   Explain that if *he, she, it,* or *you* is used alone in the subject, the verb that follows it is singular. Write these examples and discuss. *You smile. She skates. He hits the ball. It stays on the bed.* Point out that the verb following a singular pronoun ends with *-s* except when used with *you*.

PRACTICE/APPLY

Practice Reproducible   Distribute **Practice Reproducible GW37.** Read the directions and have children complete the exercises. Provide feedback.

English Learners

Third-Person Pronouns   In Spanish, speakers might omit pronouns because a Spanish verb can indicate the subject. Korean speakers might add a pronoun after the noun, reflecting a pattern in Korean: *Nathan, he is my brother.*

Answer Key: 1. *She* **2.** *It* **3.** *He* **4.** *It* **5.** *puts* **6.** *help* **7.** *floats* **8.** Sentences will vary but each should use pronouns correctly.

Singular Pronouns: *he/him, she/her, you,* and *it*

Read each sentence. Replace the underlined noun with one of the pronouns in the word box. Write the new sentence.

| he | she | it |

1. Ann plays in a band. _____

2. A nest is in the tree. _____

3. A boy waits in the line. _____

4. The book falls off the desk. _____

_____

Underline the pronoun in each sentence. Circle the correct verb. Then write the sentence correctly.

5. She (puts, put) on a hat. _____

6. You (helps, help) him. _____

7. It (floats, float) in water. _____

Write a sentence using one or more of these pronouns: *he, him, she, her,* or *it*. Underline the pronoun or pronouns.

8. _____

_____

GRAMMAR

Plural Pronouns: *they/them, we/us,* and *you*

TEACH/MODEL

Introduce the Concept   Form two groups of several children. Give each group a name: the green team and blue team. Have them stand on different sides of the room.

- Tell the blue team to point to themselves and say: *The blue team is on this side of the room* and *We are on this side of the room.* Then have them point to the other children and say: *The green team is on that side of the room* and *They are on that side of the room* and *You are on that side of the room.* Write these sentences on the board. Read them with children.

- Now hand the green team a book. Have them point to themselves and say: *The teacher gave us a book.* Then have the green team say: *The teacher gave them a book.* Write these sentences on the board. Read them with children.

Introduce Plural Pronouns *they/them, we/us,* and *you*   Reread the sentences on the board. Circle *they, them, we, us,* and *you.* Underline the nouns they replace. Explain that *they, them, we, us,* and *you* are pronouns. Remind children that the job of a pronoun is to stand for another word or words in a sentence.

- Explain that each of these words is a plural pronoun that refers to only one person or thing. (Point out that *you* can be either singular or plural.)

- Tell children that the pronouns *they* and *we* are used only in the subject, or naming part, of a sentence. Point out that the pronouns *them* and *us* are used in the predicate, or action part, of a sentence.

Introduce Subject-Verb Agreement   Explain that if *they* or *we* is used in the subject, the verb that follows is plural. Explain that the same is true when *you* refers to more than one. Write these examples on the board and discuss. *They smile. We skate. The two of you run.* Point out that the verb following a plural pronoun does not end with *-s.*

PRACTICE/APPLY

Practice Reproducible   Distribute **Practice Reproducible GW38.** Read the directions and have children complete the exercises. Provide feedback.

Answer Key: 1. *We* **2.** *They* **3.** *them* **4.** *us* **5.** *hike* **6.** *fix* **7.** Sentences will vary but each should use pronouns correctly.

Plural Pronouns: *they/them, we/us,* and *you*

Read each sentence. Replace the underlined words with one of the pronouns in the word box. Write the new sentence.

they   them   we   us

1. <u>Bill and I</u> are brothers. _____

2. <u>Sharks and whales</u> live in water.

_____

3. My father called <u>my brother and sister</u> for dinner. _____

4. The teacher taught <u>our class</u> reading.

_____

Circle the verb that belongs in each sentence.

5. They (hike, hikes) in the woods.

6. We (fix, fixes) a picnic lunch.

Write a sentence using one or more of these pronouns: *they, them, we, us,* and *you*. Underline the pronouns.

7. _____

_____

GRAMMAR

Subject-Verb Agreement: Pronouns and Verbs

TEACH/MODEL

Introduce the Concept   Have one boy and one girl stand at the front of the room. Have three children stand at the back.

- Point to the boy at the front. Say: *He is at the front.* Point to the children at the back of the room. Say: *They are at the back.* Write and read these sentences.

- Point to the boy at the front. Say: *You are at the front.* Point to the children at the back. Say: *You are at the back.* Write and read these sentences.

- Have the girl at the front clap hands. Say: *She claps.* Have the three children at the back clap. Say: *They clap.* Clap your hands. Say: *I clap.* Then have the entire group clap. Say: *We clap.* Write and read these sentences.

Introduce Subject-Verb Agreement: Pronouns and Verbs   Reread the sentences. Circle pronouns and underline verbs. Review that *he, she, I, you, we,* and *they* are pronouns. Review that *is, are,* and *claps* are verbs.

- Say: *The pronoun* I *uses the verb* am. *It also uses verbs such as* clap.

- Say: He *and* she *are singular pronouns that name one. Verbs such as* is *and* claps *are used in sentences when the subject is singular.*

- Say: They *and* we *are plural pronouns that name more than one. Verbs such as* are *and* clap *are used with these pronouns.*

- Say: *The pronoun* you *can be either singular or plural. Verbs such as* are *and* clap *are used with this pronoun.* Have children suggest other sentences using *you.*

PRACTICE/ APPLY

Practice Reproducible   Distribute **Practice Reproducible GW39.** Read the directions and have children complete the exercises. Provide feedback.

English Learners

Sentence Fragments Spanish- and Chinese-speaking children might omit some pronouns as sentence subjects because in their home languages the pronoun may be unnecessary. For example, the Spanish equivalent of *Am reading* is a complete sentence.

Answer Key: 1. *are* **2.** *dig* **3.** *is* **4.** *shop* **5.** *throws* **6.** *is* **7.** *swim* **8.** *am* **9.** *roll* **10.** *work* **11–12.** Sentences will vary but each should have a pronoun as the subject and a verb that agrees with the pronoun.

Subject-Verb Agreement:
Pronouns and Verbs

Read each sentence. Circle the correct verb to complete the sentence.

1. They (is, are) at school.

2. You (digs, dig).

3. She (is, are) the winner.

4. We (shop, shops).

5. He (throws, throw) the ball.

6. It (is, are) there.

7. They (swim, swims).

8. I (is, am) in bed.

9. I (roll, rolls).

10. You (works, work) outside.

Write two sentences. Use a different pronoun in each sentence.

11. _____

_____

12. _____

_____

GRAMMAR

Assessment

PREPARING THE TEST

- Make one copy of **Practice Reproducible GW40** for each child.
- Write the child's name and today's date at the top of the assessment.

ADMINISTERING THE TEST

- Administer the assessment to children individually or in groups.
- If necessary, read each item together with children.
- Answers are shown below. Each item focuses on the skills taught in the lesson or lessons identified.

1. Answer: flowers (Lesson 31)

2. Answer: sisters (Lesson 31)

3. Answer: bushes (Lesson 32)

4. Answer: boxes (Lesson 32)

5. Answer: men (Lesson 33)

6. Answer: children (Lesson 33)

7. Answer: *Mom <u>reads</u> a book.* (Lesson 34)

8. Answer: *Birds <u>are</u> in the nest.* (Lesson 35)

9. Answer: *<u>I</u> eat a lot of cake.* (Lessons 36–37)

10. Answer: *They <u>ask</u> for a drink.* (Lessons 38–39)

SCORING THE TEST

- Total the number of items answered correctly.
- Use the Percentage Table below to identify a percentage.
- Analyze each child's errors, using the lesson numbers provided above.
- Reteach those lessons for skills that caused the child difficulty.

Percentage Table			
10 correct 100%		**4 correct** 40%	
9 correct 90%		**3 correct** 30%	
8 correct 80%		**2 correct** 20%	
7 correct 70%		**1 correct** 10%	
6 correct 60%		**0 correct** 0%	
5 correct 50%			

Grammar Test

Write the plural of each noun.

1. flower _____   4. box _____

2. sister _____   5. man _____

3. bush _____   6. child _____

Circle the word that best completes each sentence. Then write the sentence correctly.

7. Mom (reads, read) a book.

_____

8. Birds (is, are) in the nest.

_____

9. (I, me) eat a lot of cake.

_____

10. They (asks, ask) for a drink.

_____

GRAMMAR

Verbs in the Past

TEACH/MODEL

Review Verbs   Say: *The job of a verb in a sentence is to tell what happens. A verb can tell what the subject is doing or already did.*

- Have an individual child clap. Then write this sentence, using the child's name and the present tense: *Angela claps.* Circle the verb. Say: *This is the verb in the sentence. It tells what Angela is doing.* Have another child smile. Then write: *Jared smiles.* Circle the verb. Say: *This verb tells what Jared is doing.*

- Have other children wave, walk, and jump. Repeat the routine, still using only the present tense, and circle each verb. Read all sentences with children and leave them on the board.

Introduce Verbs in the Past   Tell children that verbs in the past tell about something that happened before this moment. Explain that verbs in the past often end in the letters *-ed*.

- Point to the first sentence. Ask: *Is Angela clapping now? No. So if we want to tell about Angela clapping, we use a verb in the past.* Write: *Angela clapped.* Circle the verb. Say that *clapped* is a verb in the past. It tells about an action that happened earlier. Underline the *-ed* ending. Model forming the past tense for *smiles, waves, walks,* and *jumps*. Rewrite each sentence. Underline each *-ed* ending.

- Write these sentences: *We walked to school today. The dog barked.* Identify the past tense verbs.

PRACTICE/APPLY

Practice Reproducible   Have children complete **Practice Reproducible GW41.** Read the directions with children. Provide corrective feedback.

English Learners
Past Tense   In Chinese, Hmong, and Vietnamese, verbs do not change to show the tense. Adverbs or expressions of time indicate when an action takes place. Reinforce with children that regular past tense verbs in English always have an *-ed* ending.

Linguistic Differences
Past Tense   Many speakers of African American Vernacular English understand the use of *-ed* to form the past tense but leave it out or add sounds when pronouncing the word, as in *pick* or *pickted* for *picked*. Students will need additional work with *-ed* in order to know when and where to use it in writing. (See Linguistic Differences: Past Tense Patterns on pp. 8–9.)

Answer Key: 1. *cooked* **2.** *lived* **3.** *petted* **4.** *moved* **5.** *asked* **6.** *jumped*
7–8. Sentences will vary but each should include verbs in the past.

© Macmillan/McGraw-Hill

Verbs in the Past

Circle the verb in the past. Then rewrite the sentence, using that verb.

1. We (cook, cooked) oatmeal for breakfast.

_____

2. Jim (lived, lives) in Texas last year.

_____

3. Carla (pets, petted) a dog last week.

_____

4. My friends (moved, move) away in June.

_____

5. Yesterday I (asked, asks) a question.

_____

6. She (jumps, jumped) up from her chair.

_____

Write two sentences. Tell about two things you did in the past. Circle each verb in the past.

7. _____

_____

8. _____

_____

GRAMMAR

Irregular Verbs: *was* and *were*

TEACH/MODEL

Introduce *was* and *were* as Main Verbs Write: *Mary hops. Jon played.* Have children identify each verb. Then say: *These verbs tell what someone is doing. Is, are, was, and* were *are verbs, too. They tell what or where or who someone is.*

- Ask one child where he or she is right now. Using the child's name, write: *Gina is in the classroom.* Circle *is.* Say: *The verb in this sentence is* is. *It tells where Gina is right now.* Repeat with two children. Then write: *Lily and Marcus are in the classroom.* Circle *are.* Say: *The verb is* are. *It tells where Lily and Marcus are right now.*

- Ask the first child where he or she was before school. Repeat the routine, using *was* (for example, *Gina was at home*). Circle *was.* Say: *The verb in this sentence is* was. *It tells where Gina was before now.* Repeat the routine, using a plural subject and *were* (for example, *Lily and Marcus were on the bus*). Circle *were.* Say: *The verb in this sentence is* were. *It tells where they were before now.*

Introduce *was* and *were* as Helping Verbs Explain that the verbs *is* and *are* and *was* and *were* can also help other verbs tell what someone is doing.

- Have one child wave. Using the child's name, write: *Rosa is waving.* Circle *is waving.* Say: *This is the whole verb in the sentence*: is waving. *It tells what Rosa is doing right now.* Is *helps the verb* waving. Ask two children to smile. Then write: *Ron and Juan are smiling.* Circle *are smiling.* Explain that *are smiling* is the whole verb in the sentence and that *are* helps the verb *smiling.*

- Ask: *Is Rosa waving now? No.* Write: *Rosa was waving.* Circle *was waving.* Explain that *was waving* is the whole verb and that *was* helps the verb *waving.* Say: Was *shows that* waving *happened earlier.* Repeat with *Ron and Juan were smiling.*

PRACTICE/APPLY

Practice Reproducible Have children complete **Practice Reproducible GW42.** Read the directions with children. Provide corrective feedback.

English Learners
Irregular Verbs Many English learners need extra practice with the variety of irregular verbs that also feature unfamiliar phonics elements, such as *catch/caught, buy/bought,* and *can/could.*

Linguistic Differences
Including *is* and *are* To learn standard English, many speakers of AAVE will need to learn to retain *is* and *are* when speaking and writing. For example, students might say *He my brother.* (See Linguistic Differences: Verb *to be*, pp. 10–11.)

Answer Key: 1. was **2.** is **3.** was **4.** were **5.** are **6.** are **7–8.** Sentences will vary but each should use *is/are* or *was/were* and another verb.

Irregular Verbs: *was* and *were*

Choose *is* or *was* to complete each sentence correctly. Write it on the line.

1. A baby _____ crying last night.

2. Don _____ sleeping now.

3. She _____ a coach ten years ago.

Choose *are* or *were* to complete each sentence correctly. Write it on the line.

4. Seals _____ on the beach yesterday.

5. Now we _____ looking for shells.

6. Chris and Terry _____ not home right now.

Write your own sentences. Follow the instructions.

7. Write one sentence. Tell what is happening right now. Use *is* or *are* and another verb.

_____

_____

8. Write one sentence. Tell something that happened before now. Use *was* or *were* and another verb.

_____

_____

<u>GRAMMAR</u>

Subject-Verb Agreement: *was* and *were*

TEACH/MODEL

Introduce Subject-Verb Agreement with *was* Explain subject-verb agreement using singular nouns and pronouns.

- Write: _____ *was on the field.* Ask for a girl's name to write. Ask: *Does* Sara *name one person or more than one person?* Then circle *was.* Explain that we use *was* with singular nouns. Repeat, using a boy's name and an object such as a swing.

- Write: _____ *was on the field.* Ask: *What word could we use instead of [Sara's] name?* Write *She,* and circle *was.* Say: *We also use* was *with singular pronouns, pronouns that name only one person or thing.* Repeat with *he, it,* and *I.*

Introduce Subject-Verb Agreement with *were* Explain subject-verb agreement using plural nouns, plural pronouns, and the pronoun *you.*

- Write: *The children were singing.* Ask: *Does* the children *name one person or more than one person?* Then circle *were.* Explain that we use *were* with plural nouns.

- Write: _____ *were singing.* Ask: *What word could we use instead of* The children? Write *They* on the line, and circle *were.* Say: We *also use* were *with plural pronouns, pronouns that name more than one person or one thing.* Repeat with *we.*

- Say: *The only word that doesn't follow the rules is the pronoun* you. Point to one child. Write: *You were reading.* Point to two children. Write: *You were writing.* Explain that *you* stands for one person in the first sentence and two people in the second sentence. Circle *were.* Say: You *always is followed by* were, *even if* you *stands for only one person.*

- Summarize this information in a chart like the one shown below.

Use *was*	Use *were*
singular subject	plural subject
I	*we*
he, she, it	*they, you*

PRACTICE/APPLY

Practice Reproducible Have children complete **Practice Reproducible GW43.** Read the directions with children. Provide corrective feedback.

Answer Key: 1. were **2.** were **3.** was **4.** were **5.** was **6.** was **7.** Sentences will vary but each should use *was.* **8.** Sentences will vary but each should use *were.*

Subject-Verb Agreement: *was* and *were*

Choose *was* or *were* to complete each sentence correctly. Write it on the line.

1. We _____ pilots in the play.

2. You _____ planting seeds.

3. The tar _____ melting.

4. The teachers _____ going on a trip.

5. I _____ in the kitchen.

6. It _____ made of clay.

Write your own sentences. Follow the instructions.

7. Write one sentence using the verb *was*.

_____

_____

8. Write one sentence using the verb *were*.

_____

_____

GRAMMAR

Irregular Verbs: *has* and *have*
TEACH/MODEL

Introduce *has* and *have* as Main Verbs   Say: Has *and* have *are verbs. They tell what a person or thing owns.*

- Ask a boy to hold up a pencil. Write: *Dan has a pencil.* Circle *has.* Say: *We use* has *with singular nouns, nouns that name only one person or thing.* Ask: *What word could we use instead of Dan's name?* Write *He has a pencil.* Circle *has.* Say: *We also use* has *when the subject is* he. Repeat the routine with a girl. Modify and repeat with an object and *it.* (*The pencil has an eraser. It has an eraser.*)

- Write: *Many pencils have erasers.* Circle *have.* Say: *We use* have *with plural nouns, nouns that name more than one.* Write: *I have a pencil.* Circle *have.* Explain that we also use *have* when the pronoun is *I, we, you,* or *they.* Create the chart below.

Use *has*	Use *have*
singular noun	plural noun
he, she, it	*I, we, they, you*

Introduce *has* and *have* as Helping Verbs   Say: Has *and* have *can also help other verbs tell about the past.*

- Write: *Ann has walked home.* Circle *has walked.* Say: *This is the whole verb in the sentence.* Has *helps the verb* walked. Repeat with *She.*

- Write: *Carol and Joe have walked home.* Circle *have walked.* Say: *This is the whole verb in the sentence.* Have *helps* walked. Repeat with *They.* Refer children to the chart above for when to use *has* or *have* as the helping verb.

PRACTICE/APPLY

Practice Reproducible   Have children complete **Practice Reproducible GW44.**   Read the directions with children. Provide corrective feedback.

English Learners

Helping Verbs   The uses of *have* and *had* as helping verbs might be familiar to Spanish-speaking children once they learn the English words. The Spanish verb *haber* is used similarly.

Linguistic Differences

Subject-Verb Agreement with *do/ does* and *have/has*   Many speakers of AAVE have difficulties with subject-verb agreement when the verbs *do/does, have/has,* or *was/were* are used. Additional practice will be needed. (See Linguistic Differences: Subject-Verb Agreement, pp. 16–17.)

Answer Key: 1. have **2.** has **3.** has **4.** have **5.** have **6.** has **7.** *Sentences will vary but each should use* has. **8.** *Sentences will vary but each should use* have.

Irregular Verbs: *has* and *have*

Choose *has* or *have* to complete each sentence correctly. Write it on the line.

1. They _____ a puppy.

2. Ron _____ walked a mile.

3. The girl _____ a kite.

4. You _____ a bike.

5. The adults _____ talked.

6. He _____ the letter.

Write your own sentences. Follow the instructions.

7. Write one sentence using the verb *has*.

_____

_____

8. Write one sentence using the verb *have*.

_____

_____

GRAMMAR

Irregular Verbs: *run* and *ran*, *go* and *went*, *come* and *came*

TEACH/MODEL

Review Regular and Irregular Verbs Write: *Max walks home* and *Max walked home*. Circle each verb. Explain that *walk* is a regular verb. When a regular verb tells about one person, place, or thing, you add an -*s* to the end. When a regular verb tells about the past, you add the -*ed* ending. Then explain that you form some verbs differently. These verbs are called irregular verbs.

Introduce *run* and *ran* Write: *Max runs home* and *The children run home*. Circle each verb. Review that *runs* and *run* tell what is happening now. Point out that the -*s* is added to the verb because there is only one person doing the action. Write: *Max ran home* and *The children ran home*. Circle both verbs. Explain that these tell what happened in the past. Point out that you did not add the -*ed* ending. Discuss the spelling changes. Say: *The helping verbs has* and *have can also tell about the past*. Write: *Max has run home*. Circle *has run*. Say: *This is the whole verb in the sentence. The word* has *helps the word* run *tell about the past.* Repeat with *The children have run home*. Emphasize that you use *have* or *has* with *run*. You do not use it with *ran* because *ran* already tells about the past.

Introduce *go* and *went* Write: *Max goes home* and *The children go home*. Circle each verb. Review that *go* and *goes* tell what is happening now. Point out that -*es* is added because there is only one person doing the action. Write: *Max went home* and *The children went home*. Circle both verbs. Explain that these tell what happened in the past. Point out that you did not add the -*ed* ending. Discuss how *went* is a different word from *go*. Then explain how the helping verbs *has* and *have* are used. Write: *Max has gone home*. Circle *has gone*. Explain that this is the whole verb in the sentence. Repeat with *The children have gone home*. Emphasize that you use *have* or *has* with *gone*. You do not use it with *went* because *went* already tells about the past.

Introduce *come* and *came* Write: *Max comes home* and *The children come home*. Circle each verb. Repeat the steps above to demonstrate the spelling changes to make *came* and the use of the helping verbs *has* and *have*.

PRACTICE/APPLY

Practice Reproducible Have children complete **Practice Reproducible GW45.** Read the directions with children. Provide corrective feedback.

Answer Key: 1. *ran* **2.** *has gone* **3.** *came* **4.** *have come* **5.** *went* **6.** *have run* **7.** *went* **8.** Sentences will vary but each should use some form of *run, go,* or *come*.

Irregular Verbs: *run* and *ran*, *go* and *went*, *come* and *came*

Choose the correct verb. Then write it on the line to complete each sentence.

1. He _____ (runs, ran) a race last week.

2. He _____ (has gone, has went) to the park often.

3. Two parents _____ (came, come) to our class last month.

4. We _____ (have came, have come) to eat lunch.

5. My mother _____ (goes, went) to the dentist yesterday.

6. They _____ (have run, have ran) many races this year.

7. Sam _____ (goes, went) on a trip last summer.

Write three sentences. Use *run* in one sentence. Use *go* in one sentence. Use *come* in one sentence.

8. _____

_____

_____

_____

GRAMMAR

Irregular Verbs: *does* and *did*, *give* and *gave*, *see* and *saw*

TEACH/MODEL

Review Regular and Irregular Verbs   Write: *Manuel talks a lot* and *Manuel talked a lot*. Circle each verb. Explain that *talk* is a regular verb. When a regular verb tells about one person, place, or thing, you add an -*s* to the end. When a regular verb tells about the past, you add the -*ed* ending. Then explain that you form some verbs differently. These verbs are called irregular verbs.

Introduce *does* and *did*   Write: *Manuel does that* and *His brothers do that*. Circle each verb. Review that *does* and *do* tell what is happening now. Point out that the -*es* is added because there is only one person doing the action. Write: *Manuel did that* and *His brothers did that*. Circle both verbs. Explain that these tell what happened in the past. Point out that you did not add the -*ed* ending. Discuss the spelling changes. Say: *The helping verbs* has *and* have *can also tell about the past*. Write: *Manuel has done that*. Circle *has done*. Say: *This is the whole verb in the sentence. The word* has *helps the word* done *tell about the past*. Repeat with *His brothers have done that*. Emphasize that you use *have* or *has* with *done*. You do not use it with *did* because *did* already tells about the past.

Introduce *give* and *gave*   Write: *Manuel gives a gift* and *His brothers give a gift*. Circle each verb. Review that *gives* and *give* tell what is happening now. Point out that an -*s* is added because there is only one person doing the action. Write: *Manuel gave a gift* and *His brothers gave a gift*. Circle both verbs. Explain that these tell what happened in the past. Point out that you did not add the -*ed* ending. Discuss spelling changes. Then explain how the helping verbs *has* and *have* are used. Write: *Manuel has given a gift*. Circle *has given*. Explain that this is the whole verb in the sentence. Repeat with *His brothers have given a gift*. Emphasize that you use *have* or *has* with *given*. You do not use it with *gave* because *gave* already tells about the past.

Introduce *see* and *saw*   Write: *Manuel sees a movie* and *His brothers see a movie*. Circle each verb. Repeat the steps above to demonstrate spelling changes to make *saw* and the use of the helping verbs *has* and *have* with *seen*.

PRACTICE/APPLY

Practice Reproducible   Have children complete **Practice Reproducible GW46.** Read the directions with children. Provide corrective feedback.

Answer Key: 1. *did* 2. *has done* 3. *gave* 4. *have seen* 5. *has given* 6. *saw* 7. *have given* 8. Sentences will vary but each should use some form of *do, give,* or *see.*

© Macmillan/McGraw-Hill

Irregular Verbs: *does* and *did*, *give* and *gave*, *see* and *saw*

Choose the correct verb. Then write it on the line to complete each sentence.

1. We _____ (did, done) our homework last night.

2. Cal _____ (has done, have done) his best.

3. She _____ (gave, give) us money.

4. They _____ (have seen, have saw) the presents.

5. Ralph _____ (has gave, has given) his coat to Joe.

6. Takeisha _____ (saw, sees) Sally yesterday.

7. The teachers _____ (has gave, have given) us a prize.

Write three sentences. Use *do* in one sentence. Use *give* in one sentence. Use *see* in one sentence.

8. _____

_____

_____

_____

GRAMMAR

Verbs in the Future

TEACH/MODEL

Review Verbs in the Present and Past Say: *The job of a verb in a sentence is to tell what happens. A verb can tell what the subject is doing or already did.* Write: *Rowan waves.* Circle the verb and explain that this tells what Rowan is doing now. Write: *Rowan waved.* Circle the verb and explain that this tells about an action that happened earlier. Underline the -*ed* ending.

Introduce Verbs in the Future Say: *A verb can also tell what a subject will do in the future.*

- Say: *When I point to someone, I want that child to stand.* Point to one child. Then, using the child's name and the present tense, write: *Amos stands.* Circle the verb. Say: *This verb tells what Amos is doing now.* Repeat with another child.

- Look at another child. Ask: *What will happen if I point to Lia?* Using the child's name and the future tense, write: *Lia will stand.* Circle *will stand.* Say: *This is the whole verb. The verb* will *helps the verb* stand *tell about the future. Together they tell what Lia will do.* Point to Lia and have her stand. Repeat with other actions.

Compare Helping Verbs Explain that *will* helps other verbs tell about the future. Write: _____ *will help.* Write different singular and plural nouns in the blank. Then write the pronouns *I, he, she, it, we,* and *they.* Emphasize that *will* doesn't change when the subject changes. Remind children that *have* and *has* help other verbs tell what happened in the past, but these helping verbs change when the subject changes. Write: *I have helped* and *Kim has helped.* Circle *have helped* and *has helped.*

PRACTICE/APPLY

Practice Reproducible Have children complete **Practice Reproducible GW47.** Read the directions with children. Have children complete the exercises. Provide corrective feedback.

English Learners
Future Tense Spanish, Haitian Creole, and Hmong speakers might use present tense in places where English calls for future tense. Help children practice verbs in statements such as *I will read later* and *After we read, we will write a story.*

© Macmillan/McGraw-Hill

Answer Key: 1. *will talk* **2.** *will give* **3.** *will visit* **4.** *will walk* **5.** *will phone* **6.** *will paint* **7.** *will see* **8.** Sentences will vary but both should use *will.*

Verbs in the Future

Choose the verb that completes the sentence correctly. Write it on the line.

1. We _____ (will talk, have talked) to Bob later.

2. Mom _____ (will give, has given) me the tickets tomorrow.

3. Parents _____ (have visited, will visit) the school next week.

4. In an hour, the boys _____ (have walked, will walk) home.

5. I _____ (will phone, have phoned) Grandma soon.

6. Next week, she _____ (has painted, will paint) her room.

7. You _____ (have seen, will see) that movie next weekend.

Write two sentences. Tell what you will do later today. Tell what you will do tomorrow. Use *will* in both sentences.

8. _____

_____

_____

<u>GRAMMAR</u>

Contractions with *not*

TEACH/MODEL

Review Subject-Verb Agreement Review using *is* and *are* and *was* and *were*. Have children supply correct nouns and pronouns to complete these frames.

_____ *is outside.*   _____ *was outside.*
_____ *are outside.*   _____ *were outside.*

Introduce Contractions *isn't*, *aren't*, *wasn't*, and *weren't*   Say: *The job of a contraction is to take two words and make one word out of them.*

- Write: *Sam isn't here today.* Circle *isn't.* Then write: *is + not = isn't.* Identify and discuss the missing letter (the *o* in *not*). Explain that the job of an apostrophe in a contraction is to take the place of one or more missing letters.

- Write: *Dana wasn't here yesterday.* Circle *wasn't.* Write: *was + not = wasn't.* Identify and discuss the missing letter. Repeat the routine for: *They aren't here today* and *They weren't here yesterday.* Practice subject-verb agreement with *isn't*, *aren't*, *wasn't*, and *weren't* by modifying the frames above. Have children supply correct nouns and pronouns.

Introduce Contractions *won't* and *can't*   Write: *We can't go today.* Circle *can't.* Write: *can + not = can't.* Identify and discuss the missing letters. Repeat for *We won't go tomorrow.* Emphasize that *can't* and *won't* don't change when the subject changes. Have children supply singular and plural nouns and pronouns to complete these frames: _____ *can't help* and _____ *won't help.*

PRACTICE/APPLY

Practice Reproducible   Have children complete **Practice Reproducible GW48.** Read the directions with children. Provide corrective feedback.

English Learners

Negatives In Spanish, Haitian Creole, and other languages, double negatives (similar to *We did not do nothing*) are correct. Tell children that standard English does not use double negatives.

Linguistic Differences

Negatives Many speakers of AAVE will use several negatives in a sentence when only one is required, as in *Nobody never said nothing.* To master standard academic English, speakers of AAVE will need considerable practice to gain control of *any, ever,* and *either* after negative words. (See Linguistic Differences: Patterns with Negatives, pp. 22–23.)

Answer Key: 1. isn't **2.** aren't **3.** wasn't **4.** weren't **5.** can't **6.** won't **7.** aren't **8.** weren't **9.** weren't **10.** isn't **11.** aren't **12.** Sentences will vary but each should use a contraction.

Contractions with *not*

Write the contraction on the line. Put an apostrophe in the correct place.

1. is + not = _____   **4.** were + not = _____

2. are + not = _____   **5.** can + not = _____

3. was + not = _____   **6.** will + not = _____

Circle the two words that complete each sentence correctly. Then write the contraction for those two words on the line. Put an apostrophe in the correct place.

7. My parents _____ (is not, are not) at the park.

8. They _____ (was not, were not) home.

9. You _____ (was not, were not) on my team.

10. She _____ (is not, are not) awake.

11. You _____ (is not, are not) on this list.

Write two sentences. Use a contraction in each sentence.

12. _____

_____

_____

GRAMMAR

Contractions with Pronouns

TEACH/MODEL

Review Subject-Verb Agreement   Review when to use *is* and *are* with pronouns.

• Write: _____ *is in class.* Write the pronouns *he, she,* and *it* in the blank. Say: *With singular subjects and with these pronouns, you use* is.

• Write: _____ *are in class.* Write the pronouns *we, you,* and *they* in the blank. Say: *With plural subjects and with these pronouns, you use* are. Emphasize that *you* uses the verb *are* when it stands for one person or for more than one person.

• Write: _____ *am in class.* Ask: *What is the only word that can go in the blank?* Emphasize that *I* is the only word that uses the verb *am.*

Introduce Contractions with Pronouns   Say: *The job of a contraction is to take two words and make one word out of them. Some contractions use the pronoun* I, he, she, *or* it.

• Write: *I'm in class.* Circle *I'm.* Then write: *I + am = I'm.* Identify and discuss the missing letter (the *a* in *am*). Explain that the job of an apostrophe in a contraction is to take the place of one or more missing letters.

• Write: *He's in class.* Circle *He's.* Then write: *he + is = he's.* Identify and discuss the missing letter (the *i* in *is*). Repeat with *she is (she's)* and *it is (it's).*

• Write: *We're in class.* Circle *We're.* Write: *we + are = we're.* Identify and discuss the missing letter (the *a* in *are*). Repeat with *they are (they're)* and *you are (you're).*

• Write: *I'll come to class.* Circle *I'll.* Write: *I + will = I'll.* Identify and discuss the missing letters (the *wi* in *will*). Repeat with *you will (you'll), he will (he'll), she will (she'll), they will (they'll),* and *we will (we'll).*

PRACTICE/APPLY

Practice Reproducible   Have children complete **Practice Reproducible GW49.** Read the directions with children. Provide corrective feedback.

English Learners **Contractions** Ask children if their home languages use contractions. (In Spanish, *a + el = al* and *de + as = das.*) Explain that an English contraction uses an apostrophe to replace the missing letters.	**Linguistic Differences** **First-Person Present** In the first person present tense, many speakers of African American Vernacular English will properly use *I am* or *I'm* but pronounce it more like "uhm."

© Macmillan/McGraw-Hill

Answer Key: 1. I'm **2.** she's **3.** I'll **4.** we'll **5.** he's **6.** it's **7.** you're **8.** we're **9.** they'll **10.** you'll **11.** he'll **12.** she'll **13.** I'm **14.** You're **15.** We're **16.** Sentences will vary.

Contractions with Pronouns

Write the contraction on the line. Put an apostrophe in the correct place.

1. I + am = _____   **7.** you + are = _____

2. she + is = _____   **8.** we + are = _____

3. I + will = _____   **9.** they + will = _____

4. we + will = _____   **10.** you + will = _____

5. he + is = _____   **11.** he + will = _____

6. it + is = _____   **12.** she + will = _____

Circle the two words that complete each sentence correctly. Then write the contraction for those two words on the line. Put an apostrophe in the correct place.

13. _____ (I am, I are) at my desk.

14. _____ (You am, You are) at your desk.

15. _____ (We are, We am) at school.

Write two sentences. Use *I'm* in one sentence. Use *we'll* in the other sentence.

16. _____

_____

_____

GRAMMAR

Assessment

PREPARING THE TEST
- Copy **Practice Reproducible GW50.** Make one copy of the assessment for each child.
- Write the child's name and today's date at the top of the assessment.

ADMINISTERING THE TEST
- Administer the assessment to children individually or in groups.
- If necessary, read each item together with children.
- Answers are shown below. Each item focuses on the skills taught in the lesson or lessons identified.

  1. Answer: *looked* (Lesson 41)
  2. Answer: *were reading* (Lesson 42–Lesson 43)
  3. Answer: *has run* (Lesson 44)
  4. Answer: *ran* (Lesson 45)
  5. Answer: *have given* (Lesson 46)
  6. Answer: *will shop* (Lesson 47)
  7. Answer: *aren't* (Lesson 48)
  8. Answer: *we'll* (Lesson 49)

SCORING THE TEST
- Total the number of items answered correctly.
- Use the Percentage Table below to identify a percentage.
- Analyze each child's errors, using the lesson numbers provided above.
- Reteach those lessons for skills that caused the child difficulty.

Percentage Table			
8 correct	100%	**3 correct**	38%
7 correct	88%	**2 correct**	25%
6 correct	75%	**1 correct**	13%
5 correct	63%	**0 correct**	0%
4 correct	50%		

© Macmillan/McGraw-Hill

Grammar Test

Choose the correct word or words. Write it or them on the line.

1. We _____ (look, looked) for your hat yesterday.

2. They _____ (are reading, were reading) that book last week.

3. Jane _____ (has run, have run) all the way.

4. We _____ (ran, run) at recess last week.

5. Our parents _____ (have given, have gave) us presents.

6. I _____ (will shop, have shopped) next Monday.

7. You _____ (isn't, aren't) late.

8. Tomorrow _____ (well, we'll) see a movie.

GRAMMAR

Adjectives: Color, Size, Shape, and Number

TEACH/MODEL

Introduce the Concept Ask simple questions about familiar people, animals, places, and things. Phrase the questions so that children can describe color, size, shape, and number in their responses. Use questions such as these.

- Ask: *What color is this marker?* Say and write this sentence on the board: *It is a red marker.* Circle the word *red.* Say: *This word tells about color.*

- Ask: *What size is this desk?* Say and write this sentence: *It is a big desk.* Circle the word *big.* Say: *This word tells about size.*

- Ask: *What shape is an apple?* Say and write this sentence: *An apple is round.* Circle the word *round.* Say: *This word tells about shape.*

- Ask: *How many plants are by the window?* Say and write: *Three plants are by the window.* Circle the word *Three.* Say: *This word tells about number.*

Introduce Adjectives Say: *Some words answer questions about other words. They answer the questions, What color? What size? What shape? How many?* Write the word *adjective* on the board, and have children say it with you. Point to the words you circled. Say: *All these words are adjectives. A word that describes color, size, shape, or number is called an adjective.* Write: *I see a blue car.* Underline *blue,* and ask children to say the same sentence using other color words. Write: *We had two snacks.* Underline *two,* and ask children to say the same sentence using other numbers. Write: *I see a little dog.* Underline *little,* and ask children to say the same sentence using other words to describe a dog's size. Write: *Nora draws a square shape.* Have children draw a *round* shape, a *square* shape, a *pointy* shape, and a *curvy* shape. Write a sentence for each shape.

PRACTICE/APPLY

Practice Reproducible Distribute **Practice Reproducible GW51.** Read the directions and have children complete the exercises. Provide feedback.

> ### English Learners
> **Adjectives** Spanish adjectives have endings that match the gender and number of the nouns they modify. In Spanish and Vietnamese, adjectives often follow nouns.

Answer Key: **1.** *blue* **2.** *three* **3.** *one; round* **4.** *two; big* **5.** *small* **6.** *one* **7.** *huge* **8.** *round* **9.** *yellow* **10.** Sample Answer: The huge dog has yellow fur.

Adjectives: Color, Size, Shape, and Number

Read each sentence. Circle the adjective that tells about color, size, shape, or number.

1. The sky was blue.

2. There were three clouds.

3. One cloud was round.

4. Two clouds were big.

5. A small kite was flying.

Think about the sun in the sky. Choose an adjective from the box to finish each sentence about the sun.

yellow	round
huge	one

6. There is _____ sun. **(number)**

7. Look up to see the _____ sun. **(size)**

8. It is like a _____ ball. **(shape)**

9. The _____ sun gives us light. **(color)**

Now write a new sentence using two of the adjectives from the box above.

10. _____

<u>**GRAMMAR**</u>

More Adjectives

TEACH/MODEL

Introduce the Concept Remind children that adjectives can describe what things look like—how big, how many, what shape, and what color. Explain that adjectives can also describe what things are like in other ways. Ask simple questions about familiar people, animals, places, and things. Phrase the questions so that children can describe how things sound, feel, taste, and smell. Use questions such as these.

• Ask: *What does yelling sound like?* Say and write this sentence: *Yelling sounds loud.* Circle the word *loud.* Say: *This word tells about how something sounds.*

• Ask: *What does your desk feel like?* Say and write this sentence: *My desk feels smooth.* Circle the word *smooth.* Say: *This word tells about how something feels.*

• Ask: *What do peanuts taste like?* Say and write this sentence: *Peanuts taste salty.* Circle the word *salty.* Say: *This word tells how something tastes.*

• Ask: *What do flowers smell like?* Say and write this sentence: *Flowers smell sweet.* Circle the word *sweet.* Say: *This word tells how something smells.*

Introduce Adjectives Say: *Some words answer questions about other words. They answer the questions: How does it sound? How does it feel? How does it taste? How does it smell?* Write the word *adjective* on the board, and have children say it with you.

• Point to the words you circled. Say: *All these words are adjectives. A word that describes how things sound, feel, taste, or smell is called an adjective.* Reread each sentence to emphasize the adjective.

• Draw this chart. Discuss the items, and have children add more adjectives.

Hear	Touch	Taste	Smell
loud	smooth	salty	sweet
squeaky	bumpy	sour	rotten

PRACTICE/APPLY

Practice Reproducible Distribute **Practice Reproducible GW52.** Read the directions and have children complete the exercises. Provide feedback.

Answer Key: 1. *soft* **2.** *sour* **3.** *spicy* **4.** *scratchy* **5.** *booming* **6.** *honking* **7.** Sample Answer: warm **8.** Sample Answer: screechy **9.** Sample Answer: fresh **10.** Sample Answer: rotten **11–12.** Sentences will vary.

© Macmillan/McGraw-Hill

More Adjectives

Read each sentence. Circle the adjective that tells about sound, touch, taste, or smell.

1. I like to touch soft fur.　　**4.** I do not like scratchy clothing.

2. I do not like sour milk.　　**5.** I like booming thunder.

3. I like spicy sauce.　　**6.** I do not like honking cars.

Write an adjective to fit in each sentence.

7. I like the feeling of a _____ blanket.

8. I do not like _____ noises.

9. I like to smell _____ air.

10. I do not like the taste of _____ food.

Write two sentences. Use one adjective in each sentence. Choose from the adjectives in the box.

buzzing	soft	smelly	sharp	cold

11. _____

_____

12. _____

_____

GRAMMAR

Using *a*, *an*, and *the*

TEACH/MODEL

Introduce the Concept Write on the board: *a, an, the*. Have children read the words with you. Tell children that these words come before nouns, or naming words. Have them listen as you say each sentence below. Ask them which of the three words they hear and the noun that comes after it.

- Say: *I see the keys on my desk.* Write the sentence. Circle *the*. Underline *desk*.
- Say: *Do you need a pencil?* Write the sentence. Circle *a*. Underline *pencil*.
- Say: *Who had an egg for breakfast?* Write the sentence. Circle *an*. Underline *egg*.
- Say: *We can pick an orange.* Write the sentence. Circle *an*. Underline *orange*.

Introduce Articles Write the word *article*, and have children say it with you. Point to the words you circled. Say: *The words* a, an, *and the* are called articles. *Articles are special adjectives, or describing words.* Point to the nouns you underlined. Say: *These words are nouns. An article comes before a noun.* Say each of the rules below, and discuss the examples. Have children offer more examples.

- Use *a* before a noun that begins with a consonant. The noun should name just one person, animal, place, or thing. Examples: *a boy, a room, a playground.*
- Use *an* before a noun that begins with a vowel. The noun should name just one person, animal, place, or thing. Examples: *an elephant, an island, an oven.*
- Use *the* before a noun that names one or more particular people, animals, places, or things. Examples: *the city, the children, the books.*
- Emphasize that *an*, not *a*, should be used before a word beginning with a vowel. Have children listen for an error in this sentence and then say the sentence correctly: *I just wrote a article on the board. (an article)*

PRACTICE/APPLY

Practice Reproducible Distribute **Practice Reproducible GW53.** Read the directions and have children complete the exercises. Provide feedback.

Answer Key: 1. *An artist* **2.** *a beach* **3.** *The children* **4.** *The waves* **5.** *a boat* **6.** *a* **7.** *the* **8.** *An* **9.** *an* **10.** *the* **11.** Sample Answer: I drew a picture of an apple. **12.** Sample Answer: The apple is in a bowl.

Using *a*, *an*, and *the*

Read each sentence. Circle each article. Underline the noun that follows it.

1. An artist painted pictures.
2. One picture shows a beach.
3. The children are splashing.
4. The waves are crashing.
5. People float in a boat.

Write *a, an,* or *the* in each sentence.

6. Tyrell made _____ picture.

7. His picture showed _____ sky.

8. _____ eagle was flying high.

9. Tyrell put _____ airplane in his picture, too.

10. We like all _____ pictures by Tyrell.

Write two sentences about a picture that you drew. Use the articles *a, an,* and *the* in your sentences.

11. _____

_____

12. _____

_____

GRAMMAR

Comparing with Adjectives

TEACH/MODEL

Introduce the Concept   Use adjectives that tell about size to help children understand the concept of comparing. Draw a row of three circles on the board, each smaller than the one before. Say and point: *This is a small circle. This is a smaller circle. This is the smallest circle of all.* Have children repeat *small, smaller, smallest.* Then ask questions such as these.

- Hold up three pencils. Ask: *Which of these three pencils is shortest?* Say and write this sentence: *This pencil is shortest.* Circle *shortest.* Underline the *-est* ending.

- Hold up a thin book. Ask: *Who can point to a book that is thicker?* Say and write this sentence: *This book is thicker.* Circle *thicker.* Underline the *-er* ending.

- Have children wave their hands. Say: *Show me a slow wave. Show me a slower wave. Show me the slowest wave of all.* Write each sentence on the board. Circle *slower* and *slowest.* Underline the *-er* and *-est* endings.

Introduce Adjectives with -er and -est   Write *adjective*, and have children say it with you. Remind children that an adjective describes a person, animal, place, or thing. Write *compare* on the board. Say: *When we compare, we think about how things are different.* Point to the words you circled. Say: *Each of these words compares different things.* Point to the *-er* and *-est* endings you underlined. Say: *We add the endings* -er *and* -est *to adjectives to show differences.* Say each of the rules below, and discuss the examples. Have children offer more examples.

- Add the ending *-er* to an adjective to compare two things. Examples: *Fred is taller than Ed. (tall + -er) This plant is greener than that one. (green + -er)*

- Add the ending *-est* to an adjective to compare three or more things. Examples: *This is the sweetest pie. (sweet + -est) The cat naps on the softest pillow. (soft + -est)*

PRACTICE/APPLY

Practice Reproducible   Distribute **Practice Reproducible GW54.** Read the directions and have children complete the exercises. Provide feedback.

> ### English Learners
> **Comparative and Superlative Adjectives**
> English learners might use English adjectives in patterns from their first languages: *She was the most fastest runner. My story is less longer than yours.*

Answer Key: 1. *warmer* **2.** *quicker* **3.** *kindest* **4.** *highest* **5.** *newer* **6.** Sample Answer: softest **7.** Sample Answer: longer **8.** Sample Answer: slower **9.** Sample Answer: The strongest man in the world can lift a car. **10.** Sample Answer: The city is louder than the country.

Comparing with Adjectives

Read each sentence. Circle the adjective that compares. Then write it on the line.

1. Today is warmer than yesterday. _____

2. A cat is quicker than a mouse. _____

3. My grandma is the kindest person in the world.

   _____

4. The house is on the highest hill in town.

   _____

5. These shoes are newer than those shoes.

   _____

Write an adjective that fits in each sentence.

6. That dog has the _____ fur I have ever seen!

7. This story is _____ than that story.

8. This truck is _____ than that car.

Write two sentences that compare things. Use one adjective in each sentence. Choose from the adjectives in the box.

| strongest | colder | smaller | sweetest | louder |

9. _____

10. _____

GRAMMAR

Adverbs That Tell How

TEACH/MODEL

Introduce the Concept Say: *Every word in a sentence has a job to do. Some words tell how something is done.* Ask simple questions about familiar activities. Use questions such as these.

- Ask: *How do children play at recess?* Say: *Children play happily.* Write this sentence on the board. Underline *play.* Circle *happily.* Say: *The word* happily *tells how children play at recess.*

- Ask: *How do children work at their desks?* Say: *Children work quietly.* Write this sentence on the board. Underline *work.* Circle *quietly.* Say: *The word* quietly *tells how children work at their desks.*

- Ask: *How do friends play?* Say: *Friends play together.* Write this sentence. Underline *play.* Circle *together.* Say: *The word* together *tells how friends play.*

Introduce Adverbs Write the word *adverb* on the board, and have children say it with you.

- Point to each word you underlined. Say: *Each of these words is a verb. It tells an action.* Point to each word you circled. Say: *Each of these words is an adverb. An adverb tells more about the verb. An adverb can answer the question, How is the action done?*

- Point out that the adverb is put next to or near the verb that it describes. Also point out that many adverbs that answer the question *How?* end in *-ly.*

- Draw the chart below. Work together with children to create oral sentences for each verb and adverb, such as *Children talk loudly at recess.* Have children repeat the sentences.

Verbs	Adverbs That Tell How
talk	loudly, fast, quietly
write	carefully, clearly, neatly
work	hard, quickly, eagerly

PRACTICE/APPLY

Practice Reproducible Distribute **Practice Reproducible GW55.** Read the directions and have children complete the exercises. Provide feedback.

Answer Key: 1. *loudly* 2. *slowly* 3. *playfully* 4. *gently* 5. *cheerfully* 6. *safely* 7. *proudly* 8. *together* 9. Sample Answer: I swam smoothly across the pool.

Adverbs That Tell How

Read each sentence. Circle the adverb that answers
How? **about the underlined verb. Then write it on the**
line.

1. A bird <u>chirps</u> loudly. _____

2. A turtle <u>climbs</u> slowly onto a log. _____

3. Squirrels <u>chased</u> each other playfully.
   _____

4. A butterfly <u>lands</u> gently on a flower.
   _____

5. People <u>walk</u> cheerfully in this park.
   _____

Write an adverb in each sentence. Choose from
the adverbs in the box.

together	proudly	safely

6. Please ride your bike _____ .

7. I smiled _____ when I won the prize.

8. My friends and I play _____ .

Write a sentence about something you did. Use an
adverb to tell how you did it.

9. _____

GRAMMAR

Adverbs That Tell When or Where

TEACH/MODEL

Introduce the Concept   Say: *Every word in a sentence has a job to do. Some words tell when or where something happens.* Write simple statements about familiar activities.

- Write: *Chris went downstairs.* Underline *went.* Circle *downstairs.* Say: *The word* downstairs *tells where Chris went.*

- Write: *Then Chris ate breakfast.* Underline *ate.* Circle *Then.* Say: *The word* Then *tells when Chris ate.*

- Write: *Chris always eats cereal.* Underline *eats.* Circle *always.* Say: *The word* always *tells when Chris eats cereal.*

Introduce Adverbs   Write the word *adverb* on the board, and have children say it with you.

- Point to each word you underlined. Say: *Each of these words is a verb. It tells an action.* Point to each word you circled. Say: *Each of these words is an adverb. An adverb tells more about a verb.*

- Remind children that they learned that an adverb can answer the question *How is the action done?* Explain that an adverb also tells *when* or *where* something is done.

- Draw the chart below. Work together with children to create oral sentences for each verb and adverb, such as *The friends always talk* and *The friends talk outside.* Have children repeat the sentences.

Verbs	Adverbs That Tell When	Adverbs That Tell Where
talk	then	downstairs
write	always	here
work	sometimes	there
play	often	outside

PRACTICE/APPLY

Practice Reproducible   Distribute **Practice Reproducible GW56.** Read the directions and have children complete the exercises. Provide feedback.

Answer Key: **1.** *often* **2.** *outside* **3.** *Sometimes* **4.** *here* **5.** *Now* **6.** *indoors* **7.** Sample Answer: Sometimes I play video games. **8.** Sample Answer: I read books here. **9.** Sample Answer: I walk outside. **10.** Sample Answer: I finally finished my work.

© Macmillan/McGraw-Hill

Adverbs That Tell When or Where

Read each sentence. Circle the adverb that tells about the underlined verb. Write it on the line.

1. Mike often <u>rides</u> his bike. _____

2. He <u>rides</u> outside. _____

3. Sometimes Mike <u>plays</u> ball. _____

4. He <u>plays</u> here. _____

5. Now Mike <u>reads</u> a book. _____

6. He <u>reads</u> indoors. _____

Write a sentence to answer each question. The adverb is in bold. Use the adverb in your answer.

7. What do you do **sometimes**?

   _____

8. What do you do **here**?

   _____

9. What do you do **outside**?

   _____

10. What did you do **finally**?

   _____

Assessment

PREPARING THE TEST
- Make one copy of **Practice Reproducible GW57** for each child.
- Write the child's name and today's date at the top of the assessment.

ADMINISTERING THE TEST
- Administer the assessment to children individually or in groups.
- If necessary, read each item together with children.
- Correct answers are shown below. Each item focuses on the skills taught in the lesson identified.

  1. Answer: *green* (Lesson 51)
  2. Answer: *sharp* (Lesson 52)
  3. Answer: *an elephant* (Lesson 53)
  4. Answer: *The tiger* (Lesson 53)
  5. Answer: *older* (Lesson 54)
  6. Answer: *longest* (Lesson 54)
  7. Answer: *cried loudly* (Lesson 55)
  8. Answer: *quietly naps* (Lesson 56)

SCORING THE TEST
- Total the number of items answered correctly.
- Use the Percentage Table below to identify a percentage.
- Analyze each child's errors, using the lesson numbers provided above.
- Reteach those lessons for skills that caused the child difficulty.

Percentage Table			
8 correct	100%	**3 correct**	38%
7 correct	88%	**2 correct**	25%
6 correct	75%	**1 correct**	13%
5 correct	63%	**0 correct**	0%
4 correct	50%		

Grammar Test

Read each sentence. Circle each adjective.

1. Most trees have green leaves.

2. Pins have sharp points.

Read each sentence. Circle each article. Underline the noun that follows it.

3. Have you seen an elephant?

4. The tiger roared.

Read each sentence. Circle each adjective that compares.

5. Mark is older than his brother.

6. This pencil is the longest.

Read each sentence. Circle each adverb. Underline the verb it tells more about.

7. The baby cried loudly.

8. The cat quietly naps by the window.

GRAMMAR

Possessive Nouns: Singular

TEACH/MODEL

Review Singular Nouns   Say: *We have learned that a noun is a naming word. We have also learned that the job of some nouns is to name one person or animal.*

- Display pictures or photos showing individual people and animals or point to individual people and animals in your classroom. Avoid proper names. Have children say the singular common noun that names each one, such as *boy, teacher,* or *gerbil.* List each noun on the board, preceding it with *a, an,* or *the.*

- Reinforce that each noun is singular, meaning it names just one person or animal.

Introduce Singular Possessive Nouns   Write an apostrophe (') and an *s.* Say: *Sometimes one person or animal may have, own, or possess something. To show this, an apostrophe and an* s *are added to the noun that names the person or animal.*

- Model adding an apostrophe and *s* to each singular noun on the board. Explain that each word is now a possessive noun, or a noun that shows ownership.

- Have children name something that the person or animal each possessive noun names might have, own, or possess. Record each response beside the corresponding possessive noun as shown below. Together, read each phrase aloud.

a boy's	sweater
the teacher's	pencil
the gerbil's	cage

PRACTICE/APPLY

Practice Reproducible   Copy and distribute **Practice Reproducible GW58.** Read the text and have children complete the exercises. Provide feedback.

English Learners
Possessive Nouns In many languages, speakers show possession in phrases rather than noun endings. Show children how to change phrases such as *the tail of the cat* and *the nest of the bird* to the *cat's tail* and *the bird's nest,* in order to show possession in English.

Linguistic Differences
Possessives In standard academic English, *'s* is added to a noun to show possession. For many speakers of AAVE the *'s* is absent. However, the *'s* is regularly added to *mine,* as in *This is mines.* (See Linguistic Differences: Possessive Patterns on pp. 4–5.)

Answer Key: 1. 's **2.** 's **3.** 's **4.** 's **5.** 's **6.** 's **7.** 's **8.** 's **9.** Sample Answer: The man's pet is a bird. **10.** Sample Answer: The bird's beak is red.

Possessive Nouns: Singular

Write an ' and s beside each noun that names a person or animal. Then read each group of words.

1. a woman_____ house

2. the baby_____ rattle

3. a teacher_____ desk

4. the dog_____ bone

5. a tiger_____ stripes

6. the kitten_____ collar

7. a doctor_____ office

8. the father_____ car

Write two sentences about a <u>man</u> and a <u>bird</u>. Tell about something each one has or owns. Remember to use 's.

9. _____

_____

10. _____

_____

GRAMMAR

Possessive Nouns: Plural

TEACH/MODEL

Review Singular Possessive Nouns Write an apostrophe (') and an s on the board. Say: *We have learned that if one person or animal has, owns, or possesses something, we add an apostrophe and an s to the noun that names the person or animal. A noun like this is called a singular possessive noun.*

- Generate a short phrase, such as *the student's book*, that contains a singular possessive noun. Write the phrase on the board. Then identify the singular possessive noun and circle the apostrophe and s that end it.

- Note that the possessive noun is singular, meaning it names one person or animal.

Introduce Plural Possessive Nouns Remind children that when a noun names more than one person or animal, it is called a plural noun and will often end in s. Write *the students* on the board and identify it as a plural noun. Then write *books* after *students*. Explain that when more than one person or animal has, owns, or possesses something, and the plural noun that names them ends in s, we add only an apostrophe after the s to form the possessive.

- Underline the s that ends *students* and model adding an apostrophe after it. Have children generate similar phrases with plural nouns ending in s, such as *the bears' den*, *the firefighters' truck*, or *some friends' party*. Write them. Read each phrase and identify the plural noun. Have a child underline the s that ends the plural noun and add an apostrophe after the s to form the possessive.

- Write: *My sisters have many friends. My _____ friends are fun.* Then model filling in the blank by forming the plural possessive of *sisters (sisters')*.

PRACTICE/APPLY

Practice Reproducible Copy and distribute **Practice Reproducible GW59.** Read the text. Then have children complete the exercises. Provide feedback.

> ### English Learners
> **Plural Possessive Nouns** An apostrophe after the letter s may seem incorrect to many children. Explain the difference between clear examples such as *a cat's tail* and *cats' tails* or *a bird's nest* and *birds' nests*. Use pictures or simple drawings to help children understand.

Answer Key: 1. *girls'* **2.** *dogs'* **3.** *brothers'* **4.** *kittens'* **4.** Sample Answer: The sisters' dogs love to run. **5.** Sample answer: The dogs' leashes are red and blue.

Possessive Nouns: Plural

Read the two sentences beside each number. Then write a plural possessive noun to fill in the blank. Don't forget to use an apostrophe (').

1. The girls own many dogs.

The _____ dogs are cute.

2. The dogs have lots of spots.

The _____ spots are black and white.

3. The brothers own some kittens.

The _____ kittens are tiny.

4. The kittens have a bed.

The _____ bed is nice and warm.

Write two sentences about <u>sisters</u> and their <u>dogs</u>. Tell about things the sisters and their dogs own or have. Use a plural possessive noun in each sentence.

5. _____

_____

6. _____

_____

GRAMMAR

Possessive Pronouns: *his, her, your, my*

TEACH/MODEL

Review Singular Possessive Nouns   Say: *We learned that if one person has, owns, or possesses something, the word that names the owner is called a singular possessive noun.* Write *the girl's mitten.* Underline *girl* and circle the *'s.* Ask: *Who owns the mitten?* Reinforce that the possessive noun is singular and names just one person.

Introduce Singular Possessive Pronouns   Say: *Some words can show ownership without having an apostrophe. These words are called possessive pronouns and include the words* his, her, your, *and* my. Remind children that a pronoun is a word that takes the place of a person, place, animal, or thing.

- Display and read each sentence pair below. Identify the possessive pronoun and the noun beside it. Then identify the possessive pronoun's antecedent and draw an arrow connecting the two. Explain that each possessive pronoun is singular because it takes the place of a noun or pronoun that is also singular. Reinforce that *his, her, your,* or *my* appears beside a noun to show that someone owns it.
- Have children create other sentence pairs like those below. Write pairs. Have a child underline and connect each singular possessive pronoun and antecedent.

The <u>man</u> owns the hat.	It is <u>his</u> hat.
The hat belongs to the <u>woman</u>.	It is <u>her</u> hat.
<u>You</u> own the hat.	It is <u>your</u> hat.
The hat belongs to <u>me</u>.	It is <u>my</u> hat.

PRACTICE/APPLY

Practice Reproducible   Copy and distribute **Practice Reproducible GW60.** Read the text. Then have children complete the exercises. Provide feedback.

> ### English Learners
> **Possessive Pronouns** Asian-language children and others might try various forms for possessive pronouns—*the hat of her, you hat*—or might not always state the pronoun (*Mo Yun took off hat*). Provide additional practice.

Answer Key: 1. *her* **2.** *your* **3.** *his* **4.** *my* **5.** *his* **6.** *her* **7–8.** Sentences will vary.

Possessive Pronouns: *his, her, your, my*

**Read the two sentences beside each number.
Then underline the possessive pronoun.**

1. The girl owns a blue dress. It is her dress.

2. The toy belongs to you. It is your toy.

3. The man owns a bicycle. It is his bicycle.

4. The car belongs to me. It is my car.

5. The boy has a basketball. It is his basketball.

6. The coat belongs to the woman. It is her coat.

**Write two sentences about <u>a friend</u>. Tell about toys
that your friend has. Use *his* or *her*.**

7. _____

_____

8. _____

_____

GRAMMAR

Possessive Pronouns: *his, hers, yours, mine*

TEACH/MODEL

Review Singular Possessive Pronouns *his, her, your, my* Say: *We have learned that the possessive pronoun* his, her, your, *or* my *appears beside a noun to show that someone owns the thing named by the noun.*

- Write the sentence *It is _____ pencil* on the board four times. Have children read the sentence aloud, adding *his, her, your,* and *my.* Complete each sentence, read it aloud, and identify the possessive pronoun in it. Then, beside each sentence, complete the following sentence frame, using *you, me,* or an appropriate noun that names a person: *The pencil belongs to _____ .*

- In each pair, reinforce the connection between the possessive pronoun in the first sentence and the noun that names the pencil's owner in the second.

Introduce Singular Possessive Pronouns *his, hers, mine, yours* Say: *In addition to* his, *the words* hers, yours, *and* mine *are also possessive pronouns. These possessive pronouns are different because they stand alone in sentences.*

- Display and read the sentences below. Identify the possessive pronoun and antecedent in each pair and draw an arrow connecting the two. Explain that each possessive pronoun is singular because it takes the place of a noun or pronoun that is singular.

- Have children create other sentence pairs like those below in which *his, hers, yours,* and *mine* stand alone. Record each pair on the board. Have a child underline and connect each singular possessive pronoun and antecedent.

The <u>boy</u> owns the bat.	The bat is <u>his</u>.
The scarf belongs to the <u>lady</u>.	The scarf is <u>hers</u>.
<u>You</u> own the house.	The house is <u>yours</u>.
The game belongs to <u>me</u>.	The game is <u>mine</u>.

PRACTICE/APPLY

Practice Reproducible Copy and distribute **Practice Reproducible GW61.** Read the text and have children complete the exercises. Provide feedback.

Answer Key: 1. yours **2.** hers **3.** his **4.** mine **5.** hers **6.** mine **7.** Sentences will vary but each should use *you* or *me.* **8.** Sentences will vary but each should use *yours* or *mine.*

Possessive Pronouns: *his, hers, yours, mine*

Read the two sentences beside each number. Then write *his, hers, yours,* or *mine* to fill in the blank.

1. You own that soccer ball. That soccer ball is

_____ .

2. The blue truck belongs to my grandmother. The blue truck is _____ .

3. My uncle owns a huge sailboat. The huge sailboat is _____ .

4. The green jacket belongs to me. The green jacket is _____ .

5. The girl dropped the picture book. The picture book is _____ .

6. My mom gave me a hairbrush. The hairbrush is

_____ .

Write two sentences about something that belongs to someone. Use *you* or *me* in the first sentence. Use *yours* or *mine* in the second one.

7. _____

_____

8. _____

_____

GRAMMAR

Proper Nouns: People, Pets, and Places

TEACH/MODEL

Explain Common Nouns Say: *We learned that a noun is a naming word and that the job of some nouns is to name people, animals, and places.* Write and read *I saw a boy, a woman, a puppy, a town, a park, and a school.* Read each noun aloud and have a child tell whether it names a person, an animal, or a place. Explain that these nouns are common nouns. Point out the commas. Say: *Commas make the sentence easier to read and are used when three or more nouns come one after another.*

Introduce Proper Nouns Say: *The job of some nouns is to name one particular person, animal, or place. These special nouns are called proper nouns, and they always begin with a capital letter.* Then start the chart below.

	Common Nouns	**Proper Nouns**
People	girl	
	boy	
Animals	dog	
	cat	
Places	school	
	town	

- In the third column, model writing the name of a girl in your class. Read the name and circle the capital letter. Tell children that a proper noun names a particular girl and that it begins with a capital letter. Have children provide proper nouns for the remaining common nouns. Write them in the third column, capitalizing important words in each. Circle capital letters.

- Write and read: *I see [child's name], [child's name], [child's name], and [child's name] in my class at [your school)].* Circle commas and discuss why they are needed.

PRACTICE/APPLY

Practice Reproducible Copy and distribute **Practice Reproducible GW62.** Read the text and have children complete the exercises. Provide feedback.

Answer Key: 1. *Sarah* **2.** *Tim* **3.** *Cox School* **4.** *Oak Street* **5.** *Fluff, Sam, and Spot* **6.** *Jim, Dave, and Annie* **7.** *Smith Park, Green Pond, and Grant Zoo* **8.** *Uncle Tim, Aunt Joan, and Ellen; Franklin School* **9.** Sample Answer: I sit near Sarah, Tom, and Andre. **10.** Sample Answer: I like to visit Elm Park, Lake Tahoe, and Seattle.

© Macmillan/McGraw-Hill

Proper Nouns: People, Pets, and Places

Write each proper noun correctly.

1. sarah _____   **3.** cox school _____

2. tim _____   **4.** oak street _____

Read each sentence and underline each proper noun in it. Then add two commas that are missing from the sentence.

5. My three kittens' names are Fluff Sam and Spot.

6. Jim Dave and Annie are his best friends.

7. Her favorite places are Smith Park Green Pond and Grant Zoo.

8. We saw Uncle Tim Aunt Joan and Ellen outside Franklin School.

Complete Exercises 9 and 10. Use proper nouns to name people and places. Remember to use capital letters and commas.

9.   Write a sentence that names three people you sit near in class. _____

_____

10.   Write a sentence that names three places you like to visit. _____

_____

GRAMMAR

Proper Nouns: Days, Months, and Holidays

TEACH/MODEL

Review Proper Nouns for People, Pets, and Places Say: *We learned that a proper noun names a particular person, animal, or place and always begins with a capital letter.* Write and read: *Mom and Dad walk our dog Rex down Main Street.* Underline and say each proper noun. Ask children if it names a particular person, pet, or place.

Introduce Proper Nouns for Days, Months, and Holidays Say: *Some proper nouns name particular days, months, and holidays.* Display and read the chart below.

	Proper Nouns
Days	Monday, Tuesday
Months	January, February
Holidays	Flag Day, Memorial Day

- Reread the days and point out capital letters. Have children name the remaining days. Record them and repeat a similar process with months and holidays.

- Write and read *Independence Day will be on Friday, July 4, 2008.* Have children name and underline each proper noun, circle the capital letter(s), and tell whether it names a day, month, or holiday. Point out commas. Explain they are always added after the name and number of the day to make the date easier to read.

PRACTICE/APPLY

Practice Reproducible Copy and distribute **Practice Reproducible GW63.** Read the text and have children complete the exercises. Provide feedback.

> ### English Learners
> **Days and Months** In Spanish, French, Polish, and Vietnamese, names of days and months are not usually capitalized. In Chinese, Vietnamese, and Portuguese, names of the days are formed by counting from the first day of the week.

Answer Key: 1. *Thursday* **2.** *March* **3.** *Labor Day* **4.** *April* **5.** *Flag Day*; *Saturday, June 14, 2008* **6.** *Wednesday, November 14, 2007* **7.** *New Year's Day*; *Tuesday, January 1, 2008* **8.** *Thanksgiving Day*; *Thursday, November 28, 2008* **9.** Sentences will vary but should contain a date. **10.** Sentences will vary but should contain a holiday.

Proper Nouns: Days, Months, and Holidays

Write each proper noun correctly.

1. thursday _____   3. labor day _____

2. march _____   4. april _____

Read each sentence and underline each proper noun in it. Then add two commas that are missing from the sentence.

5. Flag Day is on Saturday June 14 2008.

6. My last birthday was on Wednesday November 14 2007.

7. New Year's Day was on Tuesday January 1 2008.

8. Thanksgiving Day will be on Thursday November 28 2008.

Complete Exercises 9 and 10. Remember to use capital letters and commas.

9. Write a sentence using the name of a day and month, the number of the day, and the year.

_____

_____

10. Write a sentence about your favorite holiday.

_____

_____

© Macmillan/McGraw-Hill

GRAMMAR

Assessment

PREPARING THE TEST

- Copy **Practice Reproducible GW64.** Make one copy of the assessment for each child.
- Write the child's name and today's date at the top of the assessment.

ADMINISTERING THE TEST

- Administer the assessment to children individually or in groups.
- If necessary, read each item together with children.
- Answers are shown below. Each item focuses on the skills taught in the lesson identified.

  1. Answer: *man's* (Lesson 58)

  2. Answer: *birds'* (Lesson 59)

  3. Answer: *my* (Lesson 60)

  4. Answer: *his* (Lesson 61)

  5. Answer: *Fisk School, Green Park, and Tom's Toy Shop* (Lesson 62)

  6. Answer: *Wednesday, June 14, 2006* (Lesson 63)

SCORING THE TEST

- Total the number of items answered correctly.
- Use the Percentage Table below to identify a percentage.
- Analyze each child's errors, using the lesson numbers provided above.
- Reteach those lessons for skills that caused the child difficulty.

Percentage Table			
6 correct	100%	**2 correct**	33%
5 correct	83%	**1 correct**	17%
4 correct	67%	**0 correct**	0%
3 correct	50%		

Grammar Test

The underlined parts of these sentences are not correct. Read the sentences. Write each underlined part correctly on the line below.

1. That <u>mans</u> dog is black and white.

   _____

2. The two <u>birds</u> beaks are big and sharp.

   _____

3. This book belongs to me. It is <u>your</u> book.

   _____

4. My grandfather owns the horse. The horse
   is <u>hers</u>. _____

5. Did you know that I visited <u>fisk school green</u>
   <u>park and tom's toy shop</u>?

   _____

6. Our new baby was born on <u>wednesday june 14</u>
   <u>2006.</u>

   _____

GENRE FEATURES

Friendly Letter

TEACH/MODEL

Introduce the Genre   Discuss these features of a **friendly letter** while reviewing and reinforcing academic language.

- A **friendly letter** is an informal letter you write to someone you know well, such as a friend or a relative. Say: *You might write a friendly letter to your grandmother or a friend who has moved away. You think about the **audience,** or the person who will receive the letter. You also think about the **purpose,** or the reason for writing the letter. The audience and the purpose of your letter can make a difference in the message that you write and the words that you choose.*

- The **heading** includes your address and the date. Say: *Your address lets the person know where to send you a letter in return. The date is the day you are writing the letter, such as April 28, 2008*. The **greeting** is the way you say hello. Say: *The greeting might be "Dear Aunt Martha."* The **body** is the message. Say: *The body might begin, "I miss you!" Then the body should tell interesting events and details*. The **closing** is the way you say good-bye. Say: *The closing might be "Love" or "Sincerely."* The **signature** is where you sign your name as the writer.

Read Aloud a Model   Read aloud this friendly letter. Discuss the questions.

> Dear Cousin Tommy,
>
>   Please come to visit soon. We could have lots of fun! The beach is nearby. We can swim and body surf. We can fly my awesome kite, too. Will you ask your mom and dad? Maybe they can come visit, too.
>
>   Sincerely,
>
>   Ron

- *Who is the **audience** for the letter?* (Ron's cousin Tommy)
- *What is the **purpose** for writing the letter?* (Ron is asking Tommy to come visit.)
- *What is the main message in the **body** of the letter?* (They could have lots of fun.)

PRACTICE/APPLY

Practice Reproducible   Copy and distribute **Practice Reproducible GW65.** Choral-read the model. Read and discuss the labels. Have partners discuss the questions and share them with the group. Provide corrective feedback.

Answer Key: 1. Danny's grandma **2.** whale-watching **3.** Sample Answer: The captain told them about whales. They saw gray whales diving.

Friendly Letter

Read this friendly letter. Study each label. Then discuss the questions below with a partner.

Heading → 20232 Santa Ana Drive
San Diego, CA 92101
March 8, 2008

Greeting → Dear Grandma,

Body →   Last week I went on a whale-watching cruise with Mom and Dad. It was so exciting!

  First, we boarded a whale-watching cruise boat. As the boat motored out to sea, the captain told us about whales. They are one of the largest animals on Earth! Gray whales swim south along the Pacific coast to find warm water.

  Then we saw a whole group of gray whales! They looked huge! We saw their spouts, backs, and tails as they dove through the waves.

  Three hours later, we returned to the dock. We were so hungry! We went to a restaurant nearby and ate fresh seafood. It tasted so good!

  We want to go again next year. We hope you'll come with us!

Closing → Love,

Signature → Danny

1. Who is the audience for the letter?

2. What is the topic of the letter?

3. What are two details that tell more about the topic?

<u>**GENRE FEATURES**</u>

Formal Letter

TEACH/MODEL

Introduce the Genre   Discuss these features of a **formal letter** while reviewing and reinforcing academic language.

- A **formal letter** is a letter to someone you don't know well, such as an adult in the community. Say: *Think about the letter's **audience** and **purpose.***

- The **heading** includes your address, so the person knows where to send you a letter in return. It also includes the date you are writing. The **inside address** is the address to which you are sending the letter. The **greeting** is the appropriate greeting for the audience. Say: *The greeting might be "Dear Mr. King." If you do not know the person's name, it might be "Dear Sir or Madam."*

- The **body** is the message. Say: *The body should begin by clearly saying why you are writing. Then it should give supporting details.* The **closing** is the way you say good-bye, such as *"Yours truly."* The **signature** is where you sign your name. Say: *The signature is your full formal name, or your first and last names.*

Read Aloud a Model   Read this part of a formal letter. Discuss the questions.

Dear Officer Lee:

   I would like for you to come talk at my school about bike safety. Many children ride bikes to school, and we want to be safe riders. Please tell us if you have time to visit. Thank you for helping us.

                                                    Sincerely,

                                                    Sophia Lopez

- *Who is the **audience** for the letter?* (Officer Lee)

- *What is the **purpose** for writing?* (Sophia wants Officer Lee to visit her school.)

- *What is the main message in the **body** of the letter?* (The children want to learn bike safety.)

PRACTICE/APPLY

Practice Reproducible   Copy and distribute **Practice Reproducible GW66.** Choral-read the model. Read and discuss the labels. Have partners discuss the questions and share their answers with the group. Provide corrective feedback.

Answer Key: 1. Sample Answer: someone at the Yosemite Valley Visitor Center **2.** Sample Answer: to request maps of hiking trails **3.** Sample Answer: The writer's family is planning a trip to Yosemite. They enjoy hiking on gentle trails.

Formal Letter

Read this formal letter. Study each label. Then discuss the questions below with a partner.

Heading →
1021 Grant Avenue
San Francisco, CA 94133
November 26, 2007

Inside Address →
Yosemite Valley Visitor Center
8701 Oak Lane
Yosemite National Park, CA 95389

Greeting → Dear Sir or Madam:

Body →
My family is planning to visit Yosemite National Park next May. We would like to hike near some of the amazing sights in the park. Please send us maps of hiking trails. We are not expert hikers, but we enjoy hiking on gentle trails.

The Yosemite Valley is such an interesting place! We are looking forward to seeing rock climbers on the huge cliffs. We also want to see the rushing waterfalls. I have seen many beautiful photographs of Yosemite Valley.

Please send the maps as soon as possible. Thank you!

Closing → Sincerely yours,

Signature → James Chan

1. Who is the audience for the letter?

2. What is the purpose for writing the letter?

3. What are two details that support the purpose?

Invitation and Thank-You Note

TEACH/MODEL

Introduce the Genres   Discuss these features of an **invitation** and a **thank-you note** while reviewing and reinforcing academic language.

Invitation   An **invitation** invites someone to come to a special event. Say: *You might send an invitation to invite your aunt to your birthday party. When you write an invitation, you need to tell the **audience** all the important things they need to know. Keep the **purpose** of an invitation in mind as you provide the following information.*

- An invitation tells the kind of **event.** Say: *You might send an invitation to a picnic or a surprise party.*
- The **date** is the day of the event. Say: *The date might be May 17, 2008.*
- The **time** is when the event begins. Say: *The time might be six o'clock in the evening.*
- The **place** is where the event will be. Say: *The address might be 2335 California Avenue, Apartment 4.*

Thank-You Note   A **thank-you note** is a note you write to thank someone. Say: *You might write a thank-you note when someone gives you a present or invites you to a special event. When you write a thank-you note, think about the **audience,** or the person you are thanking. Also think about the **purpose,** or the reason for writing the thank-you note. What ideas and words will fit your audience and purpose best?*

- The **heading** includes your address and the date. Say: *The address is your home address. The date is the day you are writing the note, such as June 25, 2008.*
- The **greeting** is the way you say hello. Say: *The greeting might be "Dear Aunt Martha" or "Dear Harry."*
- The **body** is the message. Say: *The body might begin, "Thank you for the toy robot."* Explain that the details can tell more about why the gift is special.
- The **closing** is the way you say good-bye. Say: *The closing might be "Love" or "Sincerely."*
- The **signature** is where you sign your name as the writer of the letter. Say: *The signature is your name, such as Leisha or Antoine.*

PRACTICE/APPLY

Practice Reproducible   Copy and distribute **Practice Reproducible GW67.** Choral-read the models together. Read and discuss each of the labels. Then ask partners to discuss when they might send an invitation and a thank-you note. Have them share their ideas with the group. Provide corrective feedback.

Invitation and Thank-You Note

Read this invitation and thank-you note. Study each label. Then discuss the labels with a partner. How are they similar? How are they different?

Invitation

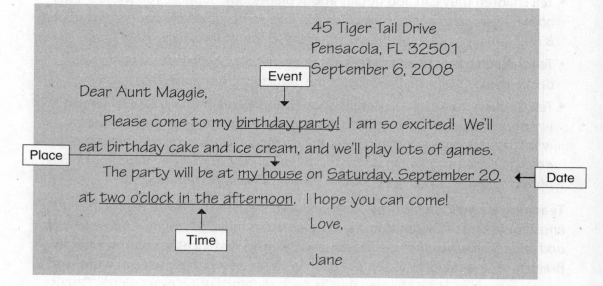

45 Tiger Tail Drive
Pensacola, FL 32501
September 6, 2008

Event

Dear Aunt Maggie,

Please come to my <u>birthday party!</u> I am so excited! We'll
eat birthday cake and ice cream, and we'll play lots of games.
The party will be at <u>my house</u> on <u>Saturday, September 20,</u>
at <u>two o'clock in the afternoon</u>. I hope you can come!

Love,

Jane

Place

Date

Time

Thank-You Note

45 Tiger Tail Drive
Pensacola, FL 32501
September 21, 2008

Heading

Greeting → Dear Aunt Maggie,

Body →
Thank you so much for the camera. I am having such
fun taking pictures! I took pictures of my puppy, Fifi, and
my kitty, Lulu. I took pictures of my baby sister, too. The
pictures are hanging in my room. You can see them the
next time you come to visit.

Closing → Love,

Signature → Jane

WRITING STRATEGIES

Adding Details

TEACH/MODEL

Introduce the Writing Strategy Tell children that good writers add **details** to make letters lively and interesting. Say: *Details can tell more about places, events, people, and things. Details can tell what the writer could see, hear, feel, smell, and taste.*

- Prompt children to choose details that their **audience** will enjoy reading.

- Tell children they can add details about places. Say: *Suppose you wrote a letter about a new pizza parlor. How could you help someone clearly understand what it is like? Could you describe the decorations you saw or the smells of the food?*

- Tell children they can add details about events. Say: *If you heard a band, what details could help someone imagine the musicians? the crowds? the music?*

- Tell children they can add details about people and animals. Say: *When you write about a person, what details are appropriate: what he or she does best? what the person says or thinks? how the person looks? You can use your senses to describe details about animals clearly. What would be the most interesting details about a giraffe?* (long legs and neck, swaying walk, patterned coat)

Teaching Using Exact Words Say: *Good writers use exact words to give the audience a clear idea of the purpose and to make letters more interesting. Choose specific and appealing words that use the senses.* Write the sentences in column 1 below. Brainstorm exact words to replace each underlined word. Write each word, and review meanings. Have children rewrite each sentence using exact words. Discuss how the new sentences are more effective. Discuss the samples in column 2.

Sentence Without Exact Words	Sentences With Exact Words
Tom wore a <u>green</u> shirt.	Tom wore a <u>wild green Hawaiian</u> shirt with <u>palm trees and flamingos.</u>
Anna was a <u>cute</u> baby.	Anna was a <u>darling</u> baby with <u>big brown eyes</u> and a <u>sweet smile.</u>
Emma knit a <u>nice</u> sweater.	Emma knit a <u>gorgeous soft blue</u> sweater with <u>seashells on the collar.</u>

PRACTICE/APPLY

Practice Reproducible Copy and distribute **Practice Reproducible GW68.** Read and discuss the directions. Then read the details and items. Have individuals complete the exercises. Then have partners discuss answers. Provide feedback.

Answer Key: 1. *spicy apple pie* **2.** *shadowy trees* **3.** *loud, jazzy music* **4.** *golden freckles*

Adding Details

Read each sentence. Add details from the box.

golden freckles	spicy apple pie
shadowy trees	loud, jazzy music

1. Don's Diner serves hamburgers and _____ .

2. The _____ towered over us in the forest.

3. The band played _____ at the concert.

4. Erin has _____ and bright red hair.

Describe a place you enjoy. Write two sentences. Include details that tell why you like this place. Think about what you see, hear, feel, smell, and taste. Use exact words.

5. _____

_____

_____

_____

_____

_____

_____

WRITING STRATEGIES

Time Order

TEACH/MODEL

Introduce the Writing Strategy Tell children that good writers tell about events in time order, or the order in which they happened. Say: *Time order helps make the events clear to the reader.*

- Say: *Suppose we wanted to write a letter about a class trip to an art museum. Let's list some things we might do on a class trip to an art museum.* List answers on the board: *Look at paintings. See sculpture outdoors. Eat lunch. Get on the bus. Ride back to school.*

- Say: *Now, how can we put these events in time order?* Work with children to number the events in the order in which they might happen.

- Say: *What time-order words can we use to show the order of the events to the reader?* Explain that you can use number words, such as *first, second,* and *third.* You can use other words instead, such as *first, next, then, last,* and *finally.*

- Rewrite the events in order, using time-order words. Have a child read them.

Teach Using Time-Order Words Write the three sentences about running in a race in column 1 below. Help children number the sentences in the right order. Then brainstorm clue words to make the time order clear. Write the sentences using time-order words in column 2, and review their meanings. Discuss how the rewritten sentences make the time order much clearer. Point out that if the last step came first, the order would not make sense.

Out of Order	In Order
I ran my hardest.	First, I warmed up my muscles.
I crossed the finish line.	Then I ran my hardest.
I warmed up my muscles.	Finally, I crossed the finish line.

PRACTICE/APPLY

Practice Reproducible Copy and distribute **Practice Reproducible GW69.** Read and discuss the directions. Then read together the events for children to number and reorder. Have individuals complete the exercises. Then ask children to discuss their answers with a partner. Provide corrective feedback.

Answer Key: Sample Answers: **1.** First, I woke up this morning. **2.** Next, I got dressed. **3.** Then I ate breakfast. **4.** Finally, I came to school. **5.** Answers will vary but should contain time-order words and be in complete sentences.

© Macmillan/McGraw-Hill

Time Order

Read the events below. Then number the events in time order, and write them in order below. Use time-order words from the box.

first	next	then	finally

I came to school.

I ate breakfast.

I woke up this morning.

I got dressed.

1. _____

2. _____

3. _____

4. _____

Write three sentences about something that happened to you. Use time-order words.

5. _____

_____

_____

Prewriting a Friendly Letter

TEACH/MODEL

Introduce the Writing Process Say: *You can follow certain steps to make writing easier. These steps are called the writing process. They help you think of what to write and how to write it. I will show you how to follow these steps to write a friendly letter.*

Introduce Prewriting Explain that the first step of the writing process is **prewriting.** This is when writers think of what they want to say. Review what writers do during prewriting.

- Writers choose a topic. They decide what to write about. For a friendly letter, first they decide on the audience, or the person who will receive the letter. Then they decide on the purpose of the letter, or what they want to tell the person. The topic is the subject they write about.

- Writers brainstorm details. They think of many details that tell more about their topic. Then they write down words and phrases to help them remember the details.

- Writers organize details. They decide which details their readers might want to read about first, second, third, and so on. They number the details in that order.

PRACTICE/APPLY

Practice Reproducible Copy and distribute **Practice Reproducible GW70.** Read and discuss the directions and the labels. Then pair each child with a partner. Provide the following support.

1. Help them choose a topic. Prompt them as needed with questions such as these. Then have children tell their audience, purpose, and topic to their partners.

- Audience: *Who will receive your friendly letter? Why are you writing to that person? What do you think that person would like to know about you?*

- Purpose and Topic: *What is the main subject of your letter? Do you want to tell about something that happened? a place you went? List events that the person might want to know about. Then choose the one you think is most interesting.*

2. Help them brainstorm events and details. Have children describe details to their partners before writing them down. Prompt them as needed with questions such as these:

- Details: *Can you think of any details about places? events? people or animals? Do the details tell what you saw, heard, felt, smelled, or tasted?*

3. Help them organize events and details. Ask: *What does your reader need to know first? second? third? Do you need to delete any extra events or details?* Have children number the events and details in the order they will write about them.

Prewriting a Friendly Letter

Plan your friendly letter by writing notes below.

Audience	Who are you writing this letter to?
Purpose and Topic	What do you think your audience would like to know about you?
Details	What are some details that might interest your audience? Write as many as you can think of.

WRITING APPLICATIONS

Drafting a Friendly Letter

TEACH/MODEL

Revisit Prewriting   Help children review the graphic organizer they completed during prewriting: **Practice Reproducible GW70.** Have them reread the events and details. Tell them that they will use these notes to draft their friendly letters.

Introduce Drafting   Explain that the next step of the writing process is **drafting.** This is when writers reread their notes and turn their events and details into sentences. Review what writers do while drafting a friendly letter.

• They write a sentence about a topic they want to tell about at the beginning of the body of the letter. They write supporting sentences in clear, logical order. They use events and details in their notes to tell more about their topic.

• They just write. They don't worry about mistakes. They will fix those later.

PRACTICE/APPLY

Practice Reproducible   Copy and distribute **Practice Reproducible GW71.** Read and discuss the page. Have children work individually to complete it, using their prewriting graphic organizer. Provide the following support as they write.

1. Help them write the heading. Say: *The heading tells your address and the date. You can use the address of your home or the school. Write today's date after it.*

2. Help them write the greeting. Ask: *What is the correct way to address the person receiving the letter: Dear Suzy? Dear Grandpa? Dear Uncle Gary?*

3. Help them draft the body of the letter. Remind them to begin with a sentence that introduces the topic to the reader. Prompt them to be specific. Say: *Exactly what event are you describing? Use your prewriting notes to add events and details in the right order.* Write the sentence frames below on the board. Prompt children to use or adapt the ones that fit the events and details they will include.

Sentence Frames

Last week, I _____ .

First, I _____ .

Next, I _____ .

Then, I _____ .

Last, I _____ .

I saw/heard/felt/smelled/tasted _____ .

I really enjoyed _____ .

---

4. Help them draft the closing and signature. Ask: *Which closing do you want to use for your letter: Sincerely? Love? Don't forget to sign your letter!*

Practice
Reproducible
GW71

Drafting a Friendly Letter

Draft your friendly letter by completing the graphic organizer.

Address

_____

_____

Date

_____

Greeting

_____

Body

_____

_____

_____

_____

_____

_____

_____

Closing and Signature

_____

_____

<u>WRITING APPLICATIONS</u>

Revising a Friendly Letter

TEACH/MODEL

Revisit Drafting   Have children reread the sentences they drafted on **Practice Reproducible GW71.** Tell them that they will revise them to make them better.

Introduce Revising   Explain that the next step of the writing process is **revising.** This is when writers reread their writing and ask themselves questions such as these: *Did I think about my audience and my purpose? Is my topic clear? Are the supporting sentences in logical order? Did I include enough details? Did I use exact words? Will the letter be interesting to the person who receives it?* Explain that when they revise, writers often vary the lengths of their sentences.

Teach Sentence Combining   Explain that good writers vary the lengths of their sentences. They write some short sentences and some long ones. Say: *One way to make a long sentence is to combine two shorter sentences using the word* but. *The word* but *is used to contrast one thing with another. The word* but *means "however."*

- Write two short sentences: *On Monday Jen went to the zoo. On Monday Fran stayed home.* Combine them to write one longer sentence: *On Monday Jen went to the zoo, but Fran stayed home.* Circle *but*. Discuss which words you included when you combined the sentences and which words you left out. Point out that the comma separates the first part of the sentence from the second part.

- Repeat with other examples. Write: *I hate mustard. I love ketchup.* Then write: *I hate mustard, but I love ketchup.*

Teach Using Commas   Explain that good writers also use commas in specific places when they write friendly letters.

- **Date** Say: *In writing the date, use a comma to separate the day from the year.* Write *April 1, 2008* on the board. Circle the comma.

- **Greeting** Say: *Use a comma after the greeting.* Write *Dear Daisy,* on the board. Circle the comma.

- **Closing** Say: *Use a comma after the closing.* Write *Sincerely,* and circle the comma.

PRACTICE/APPLY

Practice Reproducible   Copy and distribute **Practice Reproducible GW72.** Read and discuss the directions and the exercises. Have children work individually to complete them. Provide corrective feedback. When children have finished, ask them to discuss with partners the changes they made to their own papers.

Answer Key: 1. Andy is tall, but Joe is even taller. **2.** Yesterday was stormy, but today is a beautiful day! **3.** Check to make sure children revise their papers. Answers will vary. **4.** July 4, 1776 **5.** Dear Josh, **6.** Your friend,

Revising a Friendly Letter

Sentence Combining

Read each pair of short sentences. Rewrite them to make one longer sentence. Use *but*.

1. Andy is tall. Joe is even taller.

_____

_____

2. Yesterday was stormy. Today is a beautiful day!

_____

_____

3. Now find two short sentences in your letter. Combine them to make one longer sentence using *but*.

Using Commas

Rewrite each item, using commas correctly.

4. July 4 1776 _____

5. Dear Josh _____

6. Your friend _____

Assessment

TEACHER-STUDENT CONFERENCES

- If time allows, have a conference with each child about his or her writing.

- A few questions from an adult or a peer can clarify how to improve a piece of writing. Discussions often help young writers focus on audience and purpose.

- Have children read their paragraphs aloud to you. Listen attentively. Then prompt them to revise by asking questions such as those shown below.

- Try to start by identifying at least one or two things you like about the writing. Then focus on the content of what the child is trying to communicate.

- After your conference, help children decide how to revise their paragraphs.

Conference Questions

√ *Who are you writing to? What is this person like? What do you think he or she most wants to know about you?*

√ *I don't understand what happened when _____ . Could you tell me more details about that? What details could you add?*

√ *The word _____ is not really clear. Is there another word you could use? What word says exactly what you mean?*

√ *Did you double check the format of your letter? Do you have a date, greeting, body, closing, and signature? Look back at the model on* **Practice Reproducible GW65.**

- Have children proofread their papers and make neat final copies.

USING THE RUBRIC

- Use the **Scoring Rubric.** Evaluate each child's writing one criterion at a time.

- You will often find that a child's writing receives different scores for different criteria. The final score, however, should be a single number. In reaching a holistic score, give the most weight to Genre and to Organization and Focus.

- Analyze each child's errors, using the criteria and the lesson numbers provided. Reteach those lessons for skills that caused the child difficulty. **Genre** (Lesson 65; Lesson 68; Lesson 71); **Organization and Focus** (Lesson 69–Lesson 70); **Sentence Structure** (Lesson 72); **Conventions** (Lesson 72)

- Provide corrective feedback about errors in grammar, usage, and mechanics. If necessary, consider reteaching lessons in Sections 1–7.

Scoring Rubric

	Friendly Letter
Score 4	**Genre** The letter is clear and informative. The writer understands who will be reading the letter and includes vivid details that will interest that audience. Words are exact. **Organization and Focus** Writer includes the date and the proper greeting, as well as a body, closing, and signature. In the body of the letter, details are organized in a way that is easy to follow. **Sentence Structure** The writer uses both long and short sentences, as well as different kinds of sentences. **Conventions** There are not many mistakes in grammar, spelling, or punctuation.
Score 3	**Genre** The letter is clear and informative, but there may not be enough detail. Some words could be more exact. **Organization and Focus** One of the following may be missing: date, greeting, body, closing, or signature. In the body, a few details may be out of order. **Sentence Structure** Some of the sentences are short and choppy. The writer could vary sentences more. **Conventions** There are some mistakes but none make the writing hard to understand.
Score 2	**Genre** The letter is incomplete or uninformative. There are few details. Many words are vague or unclear. **Organization and Focus** Two or three of the following may be missing: date, greeting, body, closing, or signature. In the body, the details may be hard to follow. **Sentence Structure** Many of the sentences are short and choppy. **Conventions** There are many mistakes. Some make the writing hard to understand.
Score 1	**Genre** The letter is confusing. There are no details. Words are vague or confusing. **Organization and Focus** The date, greeting, body, closing, and signature may be missing altogether. **Sentence Structure** All of the sentences are short and choppy. **Conventions** Mistakes make the writing hard to understand.

GENRE FEATURES

Description

TEACH/MODEL

Introduce the Genre   Discuss these features of a description while reviewing and reinforcing academic language.

- A **description** is like a photograph in words that you can show to someone who was not there. Say: *You can write a description of a hamburger or a ride at an amusement park.* A description tells about just one person, place, or thing. This is the **topic** of the description. Say: *If I describe a hamburger, that is my topic.*

- A description includes **details** that tell what you saw, heard, smelled, tasted, or felt. Say: *If I describe a hamburger, one detail might be that it tasted juicy.*

- The first sentence tells what you are describing. This is the **topic sentence.**

- The other sentences give details that tell more about your topic. These are the **supporting sentences.**

- **Exact words** help readers picture what you are describing. Say: *A hamburger isn't wet; it's juicy.* Juicy *is a more exact word than* wet.

Read Aloud a Model   Read aloud this description. Then discuss the questions.

> I rode on an old-fashioned roller coaster. Almost everything was made of wood. Even the cars were made of wood. The seats felt splintery! The only metal parts were the tracks and the wheels on the cars and the bars that held us in. The metals bars clanked when they shut. Then the wheels creaked as the cars started creeping slowly up a long hill.

- *What is the **topic** of this description?* (old-fashioned roller coaster)
- *Which **details** tell what the writer saw?* (what was wood or metal) *what the writer felt?* (splintery seat) *what the writer heard?* (bars clanking, wheels creaking)
- *What are some **exact words** the writer used?* (clanked; creaked; creeping)

PRACTICE/APPLY

Practice Reproducible   Copy and distribute **Practice Reproducible GW74.** Choral-read the model. Discuss the labels. Explain that this model is a paragraph. Point out that a paragraph starts with an indent. Have partners discuss the questions, record their answers, and share them with the group. Provide feedback.

Answer Key: 1. a waterfall **2.** Sample Answer: *stream of water, steep cliff, rainbow mist* **3.** Sample Answer: *roaring sound, sounded like filling up a bathtub* **4.** Sample Answer: *hot, sunny day, felt damp* **5.** Sample Answer: *rocketing, roaring, drifted*

Description

Read this description. Study each label. Then discuss the questions below with a partner.

Topic

Topic
Sentence → Last summer, I saw a <u>waterfall</u>. It was a thick stream of
water rocketing off a steep cliff and falling to the ground.

Supporting
Sentence with
Details → The falling water made a roaring sound. It sounded like
someone was filling up a huge bathtub. A <u>rainbow mist</u> ← Exact Words
came off the water as it fell and drifted to the ground. It
was a bright, hot sunny day, but I put my hand on my hair,
and it felt <u>damp</u>. ← Exact Word

Supporting Sentence
with Details

1. What is the topic of this description? Find the topic sentence. Read it to your partner.

2. Which **details** tell what the writer saw? Find three.

3. Which **details** tell what the writer heard? Find two.

4. Which **details** tell what the writer felt? Find two.

5. *Rainbow mist* and *damp* are exact words. Find three more. Read them to a partner.

<u>**WRITING STRATEGIES**</u>

Describing What You See

TEACH/MODEL

Introduce the Writing Strategy   Remind children that a description is like a photograph in words. Say: *When you write a description, think about what you saw that your readers might want to know about.* Model describing what you see.

- Write: *There is a rock near my house.* Point out how this sentence does not tell readers enough. Ask: *What details can I add to describe what this rock looks like?*

- Say: *I can add details about color.* Write: *There is a <u>gray</u> rock near my house.* Discuss other color words a writer might use.

- Say: *I can add details about size.* Write: *There is a <u>huge</u> gray rock near my house.* Discuss other size words a writer might use.

- Say: *I can add details about number.* Write: *There are <u>two</u> huge gray rocks near my house.* Discuss other number words a writer might use.

- Say: *You can add details about shape.* Write: *One rock is <u>square</u>. The other is <u>potato-shaped</u>.* Discuss other shape words a writer might use.

Reread the sentences. Show how each detail created a clearer picture for readers.

Teach Using Exact Words   Say: *Exact words give readers a clearer picture.* Write each sentence below. Brainstorm exact words to replace each underlined word. Start with the exact words listed, and review meanings. Have children rewrite sentences using exact words. Discuss how the new sentences give clearer pictures.

Sentence Without Exact Words	Exact Words I Could Use
She wore a <u>pretty</u> dress.	shiny; glittering; shimmering
His shirt was covered with <u>stuff</u>.	dirt; mud; chocolate; ink
He has a <u>small</u> toy car.	tiny; teeny; itsy-bitsy; miniature

PRACTICE/APPLY

Practice Reproducible   Copy and distribute **Practice Reproducible GW75.** Read and discuss the directions. Then read together the sentences and the details in the box. Have individuals complete the exercises. Then ask partners to take turns reading aloud their descriptions of a toy. Prompt each partner to ask the writer questions about what the toy looks like. Provide corrective feedback.

Answer Key: 1. *enormous orange* **2.** *long blue* **3.** *hundreds of itsy-bitsy* **4.** *three fat brown* **5.** Answers will vary.

Describing What You See

Read each sentence. Add details about color, size, shape, or number. Use the details from the box.

hundreds of itsy-bitsy	enormous orange
long blue	three fat brown

1. He has an _____ ball.

2. We have a _____ play tunnel.

3. That game has _____ pieces.

4. I saw _____ teddy bears on her bed.

**Describe a toy you own. Write two sentences.
Include details that tell what the toy looks like.
Use exact words.**

5. _____

_____

_____

_____

<u>WRITING STRATEGIES</u>

Describing What You Hear and Feel

TEACH/MODEL

Introduce the Writing Strategy Remind children that a description is like a photograph in words. Say: *When you write a description, think about not only what you can see but also what you experience with your other senses. For example, what do you hear or feel?* Model describing what you hear and feel.

• Write: *I hear a noise outside.* Say: *This sentence does not tell readers enough. The reader does not know the kind of noise.* Ask: *What details can I add to describe how the noise sounds?* Write: *I hear a <u>loud</u> <u>barking</u> noise outside.* Also discuss words such as *buzz, clink,* and *boom* that name sounds by imitating real sounds.

• Write: *I wrap a blanket around me.* Say: *This sentence does not tell the reader enough. The reader might want to know how the blanket feels.* Ask: *What details can I add to describe how the blanket feels?* Write: *I wrap a <u>soft</u>, <u>warm</u> blanket around me.* Discuss other touch words: *hard, rough, smooth, cold,* and *prickly.*

Reread the sentences. Show how each detail created a clearer picture for readers.

Teach Using Exact Words Say: *Exact words give readers a clearer picture of what you heard or touched.* Write each sentence below. Brainstorm exact words to replace each underlined word. Start with the exact words listed below, and review meanings. Have children rewrite each sentence using one or more of these exact words. Discuss how the rewritten sentences give clearer pictures.

Sentence Without Exact Words	Exact Words I Could Use
Pam listens to <u>sounds</u> in her room.	a ticking clock; soft music; a buzzing fly
The girl has a <u>nice</u> pillow.	soft; squishy; light
In the pet store, Todd hears <u>noises</u>.	cats meowing; birds squawking

PRACTICE/APPLY

Practice Reproducible Copy and distribute **Practice Reproducible GW76.** Read the page together. Have individuals complete the exercises. Ask partners to take turns reading aloud their descriptions. Prompt each partner to ask the writer questions about playground sounds and how a cat feels. Provide feedback.

Answer Key: **1.** *splish, splash* **2.** *loud screeching* **3.** *light, soft* **4.** *rough, prickly* **5.** Answers will vary. **6.** Answers will vary.

© Macmillan/McGraw-Hill

Describing What You Hear and Feel

Read each sentence. Choose details from the box that will tell more exactly how something sounds or feels.

splish, splash	light, soft
rough, prickly	loud screeching

1. Mom listens to the _____ of raindrops on the window.

2. We hear the _____ of an owl at night.

3. I tickle my friend with a _____ feather.

4. Dan scraped his arm on the _____ rose bush.

Read the directions. Write sentences.

5. Describe sounds you hear on the school playground. Write two sentences. Use exact words.

_____

_____

_____

6. Describe what a cat feels like when you pet it. Write two sentences. Use exact words.

_____

_____

WRITING STRATEGIES

Describing What You Smell and Taste

TEACH/MODEL

Introduce the Writing Strategy   Remind children that a description is like a photograph in words. Say: *The writer can use the five senses—those of sight, sound, touch, taste, and smell—to make a description come alive for the reader.*

- Write: *Mom's perfume smells like sweet flowers.* Say that comparing the perfume to a smell they are familiar with can help them to write a better description. Repeat the routine with this sentence: *The awful smell was like burnt toast.*

- Write: *The crackers taste good.* Say: *This sentence does not tell readers enough.* Write: *The crackers taste salty.* Explain that this gives readers a more exact idea of how the crackers tasted. Repeat with *The peach is good.* Write: *The peach is sweet.*

Reread the sentences. Show how each detail creates a clearer picture for readers.

Teach Comparing with Exact Words   Say: *Comparing smells and tastes with familiar things makes descriptions clearer.* Write each sentence below. Add the comparison and rewrite the sentence. Discuss how the new sentence gives a clearer picture. Brainstorm other comparisons for each smell or taste.

How It Smells or Tastes	Compares With
The forest smells fresh.	like a Christmas tree
The peach tastes sweet.	like candy
My juice tastes sour.	like a lemon
The room smells rotten.	like garbage

Say: *Some smells and tastes are good, and some are bad. The words* good *and* bad *are not exact; they do not give enough information.* Write: _____ *smells good.* _____ *tastes good.* Have children name things that smell and taste good. Have them replace *good* with an exact smell or taste. Repeat for a bad smell and taste.

PRACTICE/APPLY

Practice Reproducible   Copy and distribute **Practice Reproducible GW77.** Read and discuss the page. Have individuals complete the exercises. Ask partners to take turns reading aloud their riddle descriptions. Provide corrective feedback.

Answer Key: 1. *stinky* **2.** *sweet* **3.** *sour* **4.** *creamy* **5–6.** Answers will vary.

Describing What You Smell and Taste

Replace the underlined word with a more exact smell or taste from the box. Write the exact word on the line.

| sweet | sour | creamy | stinky |

1. A skunk can have a <u>bad</u> smell. _____

2. The roses in the garden smell <u>great</u>. _____

3. I don't like to drink <u>bad</u> milk. _____

4. The ice cream tastes <u>good</u>. _____

Write two riddles for a partner to guess. One riddle should include a taste clue and the other a smell clue. You may add other clues as well.

Example: I feel cold and taste minty. You eat me in a cone. What am I?

5. I taste _____ . You eat me _____

_____ . What am I?

6. I smell _____ . You smell me _____

_____ . What am I?

WRITING STRATEGIES

Topic Sentences

TEACH/MODEL

Introduce the Writing Strategy   Remind children that a description tells about just one person, place, or thing, which is the topic. The first sentence tells what you are describing. This is the **topic sentence.**

Read Aloud a Model   Read aloud this description. Then discuss how the topic sentence is missing and suggest topic sentences that the writer could have used.

> The circus music was loud and jazzy as the parade began. I laughed at two fat clowns with funny red noses. My family clapped for all the acts. My sister liked the small dogs and the big lions doing tricks. The seats felt hard, but I didn't mind. We smelled buttery popcorn, so Dad bought some for all of us. It tasted salty. We had a great time!

- Say: *The sentences in the description tell details about one topic or thing. What is the topic?* Explain that the topic sentence, which tells what is being described, is missing.

- *Now we need to think of one sentence that tells about all the other sentences in the description.* Write: *The circus was an exciting place.* Ask children if this is a good topic sentence and why or why not. (*Yes, because all the sentences describe the circus and make it seem like an exciting place.*)

- Tell children the topic sentence could also be written as a question. Write: *Do you think the circus is an exciting place?*

- Explain that the topic sentence might also be written with an exclamation point to show excitement. Write: *The circus was an exciting place!*

- Tell children that there may be more than one possible topic sentence for a paragraph, but it must tell what all the other sentences are describing. Have children suggest other topic sentences. (*My family likes to go to the circus. I was amazed by everything at the circus! Did you go to see the circus?*)

PRACTICE/APPLY

Practice Reproducible   Copy and distribute **Practice Reproducible GW78.** Choral-read each description together. Read and discuss the directions. Then read together each paragraph. Have individuals complete the exercises. Have partners share their answers. Provide corrective feedback.

Answer Key: 1. My family had fun camping. **2.** Sample Answer: It was interesting to watch animals in the pet store. **3.** Sample Answer: My family stills talks about how camping was fun! **4.** Sample Answer: My trip to the pet store wasn't boring!

Topic Sentences

Read this description. Choose the best topic sentence from the box, and write it on the line.

My family saw two deer. My family had fun camping.

1. _____
_____ Dad put up two big tents.
Then we went swimming in the lake. The water
felt cold. Later, Mom made a campfire to cook our
food. Afterward, our clothes smelled smoky. We
ate juicy hotdogs. In our sleeping bags at night,
my sister was afraid of a screeching owl.

Read this description. Write your own topic sentence on the line.

2. _____
_____ Animals were
everywhere in the store. Dogs were barking. A
boy was petting a soft black kitten. One part of
the store smelled fishy. That was where all the fish
tanks were. A little girl fed some crackers to the
parrots. A mouse squeaked and ran on its wheel.

Write each topic sentence above another way.

3. _____

4. _____

<u>**WRITING STRATEGIES**</u>

Avoiding Extra Details

TEACH/MODEL

Introduce the Writing Strategy   Remind children that all the details in a description should tell about the topic. Say: *When rereading a description you wrote, check that all the details about what you saw, heard, smelled, tasted, or felt relate to one topic or to what you described.*

Read Aloud a Model   Read aloud this description. Say: *Some of the sentences do not belong because they tell about details not related to the topic.* Then discuss the questions.

> Jane likes to shop in the food store with her mom. The store has long rows of food on shelves. It has carts to put your food in. The cart feels cold, and its wheels are squeaky. Mom and Jane fill the cart with juicy fruit, meat, boxes of rice, and canned goods. Jane likes to draw pictures of food. Mom pays for the food at the checkout counter. Yesterday, they went to the clothing store.

- *What is the topic of this description?* (shopping at a food store)
- *What two sentences do not belong because they do not tell details about the food store?* (Jane likes to draw pictures of food. Yesterday, they went to the clothing store.)
- Reread the description, leaving out the sentences that don't belong. Then invite children to suggest other sentences that could be added to the description to tell more about the topic of shopping at a food store.

PRACTICE/APPLY

Practice Reproducible   Copy and distribute **Practice Reproducible GW79.** Read and discuss the directions. Explain that each description is written as a paragraph. Point out that a paragraph starts with an indent. Then read together one description at a time. Have individuals complete the exercises. Then have partners share which sentences they deleted and tell why. Provide corrective feedback.

Answer Key: 1. Delete sentences: *I will go shopping for new shirts and pants today. I also like spicy pizza.* **2.** Delete sentences: *My friend next door has airplane models. You need to use glue to make airplane models.*

© Macmillan/McGraw-Hill

Avoiding Extra Details

Read the two descriptions. Then cross out any sentences with extra details that do not tell about the topic.

Description 1:

My bedroom is my own special place. I have a short dresser for my clothes. I will go shopping for new shirts and pants today. My bed has a purple quilt on it. I have a CD player in my bedroom. I like to play soft music on it when I go to sleep. I also like spicy pizza. The rug is smooth and feels warm on my bare feet. I have a tall bookcase for toys and books. I like to be in my bedroom with friends or alone.

Description 2:

I collect teddy bears. I have black, brown, and white bears. They are short and tall. One bear is named Ted. He is soft, fat, and furry. I have a small bear with a silky blouse. My friend next door has airplane models. You need to use glue to make airplane models. You can press one paw of my polar bear and hear a growling sound. All my teddy bears are my friends.

WRITING APPLICATIONS

Prewriting a Description

TEACH/MODEL

Introduce the Writing Process   Say: *You can follow certain steps to make writing easier. These steps are called the writing process. They help you think of what to write and how to write it. I will show you how to follow these steps to write a description.*

Introduce Prewriting   Explain that the first step of the writing process is **prewriting.** This is when writers think of what they want to say. Review what writers do during prewriting.

• Writers choose a topic. They decide what to write about.

• Writers brainstorm details. They think of many details that tell more about their topic. Then they write down words and phrases to help them remember.

• Writers organize details. They decide which details their readers might want to read about first, second, third, and so on. They number the details in that order.

PRACTICE/APPLY

Practice Reproducible   Copy and distribute **Practice Reproducible GW80.** Read and discuss the directions and the labels on the graphic organizer. Make sure children understand that they don't have to complete any rows that don't fit their topic, such as taste or smell. Then pair each child with a partner. Provide the following support.

1. Help them choose a topic. Have children tell their topic to their partner. Ask: *Do you remember enough about this topic? Can you describe it using at least three of your five senses? Is the topic too big? Do you need to describe a smaller part of it?*

2. Help them brainstorm details. Have children read each label on the graphic organizer and describe each kind of detail orally to their partner before writing down any details. Prompt them as needed with questions such as these:

• What It Looked Like *What shape was it? What size? Was it one color or more than one color?*

• What It Sounded Like *Did it make any noises? What exactly did those noises sound like? Were they loud or soft?*

• What It Felt Like *Did you feel it? Was it smooth or rough? soft or hard?*

• What It Smelled Like *Did it have a smell? What did it smell like? Was it a pleasant smell or an unpleasant smell? a strong smell or a smell you hardly noticed?*

• What It Tasted Like *Did you taste it? What did it taste like?*

3. Help them organize details. Ask: *What does your reader need to know first? second? third? Do you need to delete any extra details?* Have them number the details in the order they will write about them.

Practice
Reproducible
GW80

Prewriting a Description

Write your topic. Then write details about your topic. Add details to as many rows as you can.

My Topic _____

What It Looked Like	
What It Sounded Like	
What It Felt Like	
What It Smelled Like	
What It Tasted Like	

<u>**WRITING APPLICATIONS**</u>

Drafting a Description

TEACH/MODEL

Revisit Prewriting   Help children review the graphic organizer they completed during prewriting: **Practice Reproducible GW80.** Have them reread the details they wrote. Tell them that they will use these details to draft their descriptions.

Introduce Drafting   Explain that the next step of the writing process is **drafting.** This is when writers reread their graphic organizers and turn their details into sentences. Review what writers do during drafting.

- They write a topic sentence. They write one sentence that tells exactly what they are describing.
- They write supporting sentences. They use the details in their graphic organizer to write sentences that tell more about their topic.
- They just write. They don't worry about mistakes. They will fix these later.

PRACTICE/APPLY

Practice Reproducible   Copy and distribute **Practice Reproducible GW81.** Read and discuss the directions and the labels. Then have children work individually to complete it. Circulate around the room. Remind children to use the details they wrote on their prewriting graphic organizers. Provide the following support as children write.

1. Help them write a topic sentence. Help children complete the sentence frame. Prompt them to be as specific as possible about their topic. Ask questions such as these: *What kind of place are you describing? Is it a park? someone's yard?*

2. Help them write supporting sentences. Write the sentence frames below on the board. Prompt children to use or adapt the ones that fit the details they decide to include.

Sentence Frames
It has a _____ color.
Part of it is shaped like a _____ .
Another part is shaped like a _____ .
I heard it making a noise that sounded _____ .
When I touched it, it felt _____ .
When I sniffed, it smelled _____ .
It tasted _____ .

© Macmillan/McGraw-Hill

Drafting a Description

Write a sentence in each box. Use the details you wrote during prewriting.

Topic Sentence

I will describe _____

↓

Supporting Sentence #1

_____

_____

↓

Supporting Sentence #2

_____

_____

↓

Supporting Sentence #3

_____

_____

Revising a Description

TEACH/MODEL

Revisit Drafting   Have children reread the sentences they drafted on **Practice Reproducible GW81.** Tell them that they will revise these sentences to make them better.

Introduce Revising   Explain that the next step of the writing process is **revising.** This is when writers reread their writing and ask themselves questions such as these: *Did I write a topic sentence and supporting sentences? Did I include enough details? Did I use exact words?* Explain that when they revise, writers often vary their sentences.

Teach Sentence Combining   Explain that good writers vary the lengths of their sentences. They write some short sentences and some long ones. Say: *One way to make a long sentence is to combine two shorter sentences using the word* and.

- Write two short sentences: *The house is large. It is shaped like a square.* Combine them to write one longer sentence: *The house is large and shaped like a square.*

- Circle *and.* Discuss what words you included when you combined the sentences and what words you left out.

- Repeat with other examples. Write: *I came to school late. I forgot my homework.* Then write: *I came to school late, and I forgot my homework.*

Teach Using Different Kinds of Sentences   Explain that good writers also vary the kinds of sentences they use. They might rewrite a statement as an interrogative.

- Write: *I never saw a pink and orange car before.* Say: *This is a statement. It is one kind of sentence.* Circle the period.

- Then write: *Have you ever seen a pink and orange car before?* Say: *This is an interrogative. This kind of sentence asks a question.* Circle the question mark.

- Repeat with other examples. Write: *I wish I could eat ice cream every day.* Then write: *Don't you wish you could eat ice cream every day?*

PRACTICE/APPLY

Practice Reproducible   Copy and distribute **Practice Reproducible GW82.** Read and discuss the directions and the exercises. Have children work individually to complete them. Circulate and provide corrective feedback. When children have finished, have them discuss with a partner the changes they made.

Answer Key: 1. The book was thick and heavy as a rock. **2.** The stairs were narrow and dark. **3.** Answers will vary. **4.** Sample Answer: Have you ever been to an amusement park? **5.** Answers will vary.

© Macmillan/McGraw-Hill

Revising a Description

Sentence Combining

**Read each pair of short sentences. Rewrite them
to make one longer sentence. Use *and*.**

1. The book was thick. It was as heavy as a rock.

_____

_____

2. The stairs were narrow. They were dark.

_____

_____

3. Now find two short sentences in your description.
Combine them to make one longer sentence
using *and*.

Using Different Kinds of Sentences

Rewrite this sentence as an interrogative.

4. I have never been to an amusement park.

_____

_____

5. Change one statement in your description to an
interrogative.

Assessment

TEACHER-STUDENT CONFERENCES

- If time allows, have a conference with each child about his or her writing.

- A few questions from an adult or a peer can clarify how to improve a piece of writing. Discussions can help young writers focus on audience and purpose.

- Have children read their paragraphs to you. Listen attentively. Then prompt them to revise by asking questions such as those shown below.

- Try to start by identifying at least one or two things you like about the writing. Then focus on the content of what the child is trying to communicate.

- After your conference, help children decide how to revise their paragraphs.

Conference Questions

√ *What topic are you telling me about? Do all your facts tell about just this one topic?*

√ *You told me some interesting facts about _____ . What else did you learn about this?*

√ *The word _____ is not really clear. Is there another word you could use? What word says exactly what you mean?*

√ *When you first started reading, I wasn't sure what topic you were writing about. Can you make that clear in the first sentence? Look back at the topic sentence in the model on* **Practice Reproducible GW74.**

- Have children proofread their papers and make neat final copies.

USING THE RUBRIC

- Use the **Scoring Rubric.** Evaluate each child's writing one criterion at a time.

- You will often find that a child's writing receives different scores for different criteria. The final score, however, should be a single number. In reaching a holistic score, give the most weight to Genre and to Organization and Focus.

- Analyze each child's errors using the criteria and the lesson numbers provided. Reteach those lessons for skills that caused the child difficulty.

  Genre (Lesson 74–Lesson 77; Lesson 81)

  Organization and Focus (Lesson 78–Lesson 80)

  Sentence Structure (Lesson 82)

  Conventions (Lesson 82)

- Provide corrective feedback about errors in grammar, usage, and mechanics. If necessary, consider reteaching lessons in Sections 1–7.

Scoring Rubric

	Descriptive Paragraph
Score 4	**Genre** The writer describes one person, place, or thing. Many details tell what the writer saw, heard, felt, smelled, or tasted. Exact, interesting words help readers picture what is described. **Organization and Focus** A topic sentence tells exactly what the writer is describing. Supporting sentences include only details that tell more about the topic. **Sentence Structure** The writer uses both long and short sentences, as well as different kinds of sentences. **Conventions** There are few mistakes in grammar, spelling, or punctuation.
Score 3	**Genre** The writer describes one person, place, or thing but may need to tell more about what he or she saw, heard, felt, smelled, or tasted. Some words could be more exact. **Organization and Focus** The topic sentence may not tell exactly what is being described. Supporting sentences may include a few extra details that do not tell more about the topic. **Sentence Structure** Some of the sentences are short and choppy. The writer could vary sentences more. **Conventions** There are some mistakes but none make the writing hard to understand.
Score 2	**Genre** The writer does not describe only one thing. Many details are missing. The writer tells very little about what he or she saw, heard, felt, smelled, or tasted. Many words are vague or unclear. **Organization and Focus** The topic sentence is confusing or misleading. Supporting sentences include many extra details that do not tell more about the topic. **Sentence Structure** Many of the sentences are short and choppy. **Conventions** There are many mistakes. Some make the writing hard to understand.
Score 1	**Genre** The topic is not clear. There are no details. Words are vague or confusing. **Organization and Focus** There is no topic sentence. Supporting sentences are missing. **Sentence Structure** All sentences are short and choppy. **Conventions** Mistakes make the writing hard to understand.

GENRE FEATURES

Autobiographical Narrative

TEACH/MODEL

Introduce the Genre Discuss these features of an autobiographical narrative.

- A **narrative** is a story with a beginning, a middle, and an end.

- An **autobiographical** narrative tells a story about something that happened to the writer. Say: *If my family went to the beach, I could write a story about that. The beginning could be when we first got to the beach; the middle, what we did at the beach; and the end, when we left the beach.*

- An autobiographical narrative should tell about one **event,** one thing that happened. Say: *If I was writing about a trip to the beach, I wouldn't also write about something that happened on another trip.*

- Say: *Because the story is about you, use the word* I *to talk about yourself.*

- Readers like specific **details** that tell about the event. Say: *If my story takes place on a beach, one detail might describe ocean waves crashing on the shore. I would include other details that help explain why this is important to me.*

Read Aloud a Model Read aloud this autobiographical narrative. Then discuss.

> My aunt and uncle took me to a park in their city. The park had a special building made of fences and netting. The building was filled with parakeets! We walked inside. At first, I was scared because parakeets were flying everywhere. Then one landed on my shoulder! I held up some birdseed. The parakeet ate it. When the food was all gone, the parakeet flew away. After that, I wasn't afraid of birds anymore.

Discussion Questions *What* **event** *does the writer choose to write about?* (a visit to a parakeet building) *Which sentences describe the beginning of the event?* (first three sentences) *Why is the event important to the writer?* (not afraid of birds anymore)

PRACTICE/APPLY

Practice Reproducible Copy and distribute **Practice Reproducible GW84.** Choral-read the model together. Read and discuss each label. Explain that this model is a paragraph. Have partners discuss the questions. Have them record their answers and then share them with the group. Provide corrective feedback.

Answer Key: 1. Sample Answer: a walk on the beach where his dog wrecked a tower **2.** first sentence **3.** / **4.** They were upset. **5.** Sample Answers: *spied; scattering; destroyed* **6.** Sample Answer: *I built the tower again, exactly the way it was before.* The writer fixed what someone else had made that the dog destroyed.

Autobiographical Narrative

Read this autobiographical narrative. Study each label. Then discuss the questions below with a partner.

Beginning → My family and I were walking on the beach with my dog, Milo. From far away, we spied something strange. When we got close, we saw that it was a tiny tower. <u>Someone had</u> ← Detail <u>built it from stones, seashells, and bird feathers.</u> Suddenly

Middle — Milo began running and barking. He <u>charged</u> into the tower, ← Exact Words scattering everything. It was destroyed! Mom and Dad were upset. I remembered how the tower had looked. I collected the stones, shells, and feathers. I built the tower again, exactly the way it was before. I felt very happy. ← End

1. What one event is this autobiographical narrative about? Discuss it with your partner.

2. Which sentence tells the beginning of this event? Read it to your partner.

3. Which pronoun does the writer use to tell the story?

4. Which detail tells what the parents felt?

5. *Charged* is an exact word. Find three more. Read them to a partner.

6. Which sentence tells the ending of this event? Why is the event important to the writer? Discuss this with your partner.

Remembering an Event

TEACH/MODEL

Introduce the Writing Strategy   Remind children that an autobiographical narrative tells a story about something that happened to them. Say: *Before you write an autobiographical narrative, you need to remember an event that would make a good story.* Follow these steps to model remembering an event.

- The first step is to list interesting events. Say: *I remember when my brother got lost in an airport, when I dropped my watch in a dumpster, and when a cloud in the sky looked like a turtle.* List these: *brother in airport, watch, turtle cloud.*

- An autobiographical narrative tells about an event that happened to the writer. Say: *I'm going to put a check next to the events that happened to me and cross out events that happened to someone else.* Cross out *brother in airport.*

- It also has a beginning, a middle, and an end. Put another check by *watch.* Say: *This story could have a beginning, a middle, and an end.* Cross out *turtle cloud* as you say: *There's no story here. There's no beginning, middle, or end.*

- Say: *The dumpster story has a beginning, a middle, and an end. I could tell about how my watchband broke and how I held it while trying to throw out trash.*

Model Remembering the Beginning, Middle, and End   Create a graphic organizer like the following, and model completing it for one of these events.

I remember when I dropped my watch in a dumpster.
What happened in the beginning? My watchband broke, so I had to carry my watch in my hand.
What happened in the middle? My mom asked me to take out the trash, and I accidentally threw my watch in the dumpster with the trash.
What happened in the end? My mom got it out for me.

PRACTICE/APPLY

Practice Reproducible   Distribute **Practice Reproducible GW85.** Then pair each child with a partner. Provide the following support.

1. Help children write their topics. Have children tell a partner about events they remember. Have partners discuss which events would make good stories.

2. Help them identify beginning, middle, and end. Have children describe the beginning, middle, and end to their partner before writing down details.

Practice
Reproducible
GW85

Remembering an Event

I remember when _____

What happened in the beginning?

What happened in the middle?

What happened in the end?

I remember when _____

What happened in the beginning?

What happened in the middle?

What happened in the end?

WRITING STRATEGIES

Adding Details About a Place

TEACH/MODEL

Introduce the Writing Strategy Remind children that adding details to an autobiographical narrative helps readers paint pictures in their mind. Say: *When you add details, think about what readers might want to know about where your story takes place.* Then model adding details about a place.

- Write: *We went to a campsite.* Point out how this sentence does not tell readers enough. Ask: *What details can I add to help my readers picture this campsite?*

- Say: *I can add details about what the campsite looked like.* Write: *The campsite had two picnic tables.* Discuss other visual details a writer might add.

- Say: *I can add details about what I heard.* Write: *I heard the roar of motorboats on the lake.* Discuss other details about sounds that a writer might add.

- Say: *I can add details about what I smelled.* Write: *I smelled the tomato sauce Dad was cooking.* Discuss other details about smells that a writer might add.

- Say: *I can add details about what I tasted.* Write: *I tasted the tart blueberries in Mom's pancakes.* Discuss other details about taste that a writer might add.

- Say: *I can add details about what I felt.* Write: *I felt pine needles under my feet.* Discuss other details about touch or feel that a writer might add.

Point out how each detail you added created a clearer picture for readers.

Teach Using Exact Words Say: *Exact words give readers a clearer picture of what you saw, heard, smelled, tasted, or felt in the place you are writing about.* Write each sentence below. Have children rewrite each sentence using exact words. Start with the list below. Discuss how the rewritten sentences paint clearer pictures.

Sentence Without Exact Words	Exact Words I Could Use
The sauce tasted <u>good</u>.	peppery; spicy; salty
We put a <u>nice</u> tarp over our tent.	blue; waterproof; shiny
I heard <u>sounds</u> from another tent.	music; voices; barking

PRACTICE/APPLY

Practice Reproducible Distribute **Practice Reproducible GW86.** Read the directions. Have individuals complete the exercises. Then have partners take turns reading aloud the details they wrote about a place. Provide feedback.

Answer Key: 1. *soft wool* **2.** *hot and spicy* **3.** *of something banging* **4.** *of burning leaves* **5.** *with blue light* **6.** Sentences should use details to describe a room.

Adding Details About a Place

Read each sentence. Add details about sight, sound, smell, taste, and touch. Use the details from the box.

of burning leaves	with blue light
hot and spicy	soft wool
of something banging	

1. We felt the _____ blankets in the bedroom.

2. In the kitchen, I tasted the _____ soup.

3. We heard the sound _____ in the washing machine.

4. The smell _____ came through the windows.

5. Two lamps filled the living room _____
   _____ .

Write two sentences. Describe the room you are in right now. Include details about how this place looks, sounds, smells, tastes, or feels. Use exact words.

6. _____
   _____
   _____

WRITING STRATEGIES

Adding Details About People

TEACH/MODEL

Introduce the Writing Strategy Remind children that adding details to an autobiographical narrative helps readers see and hear things the way the writer saw and heard them. Say: *When you add details, think about what your readers might want to know about how people looked, sounded, and acted.*

- Write: *The girl went to the playground.* Point out how this sentence does not tell readers enough. Ask: *What details can I add about the girl?*

- Say: *I can add details about what the girl looked like.* Write: *The girl in green sneakers went to the playground.* Discuss other details a writer might add about what the girl looked like.

- Say: *I can add details about how the girl sounded as she went to the playground.* Write: *Singing all the way, the girl in green sneakers went to the playground.* Discuss other details a writer might add about how the girl sounded.

- Say: *I can add details about what the girl did.* Write: *Singing all the way, the girl in green sneakers rode her bike to the playground.* Discuss other details a writer might add about what the girl did.

Point out how each detail you added created a clearer picture for the reader.

Teach Comparing with Exact Words Say: *Exact words give readers a clearer picture of how people looked, sounded, and acted.* Write each sentence below. Then brainstorm exact words to replace each underlined word. Start with the exact words listed below. Discuss how the rewritten sentences are clearer.

Sentence Without Exact Words	Exact Words I Could Use
Jim looked <u>good</u>.	neat; handsome; rested
They sounded <u>bad</u>.	tired; sad; upset
The friends <u>went</u> home.	raced; skipped; jogged

PRACTICE/APPLY

Practice Reproducible Distribute **Practice Reproducible GW87.** Read the directions. Have individuals complete the exercises. Then ask partners to take turns reading aloud the details they wrote. Provide corrective feedback.

Answer Key: 1. *with purple feathers* **2.** *did cartwheels* **3.** *in a very loud voice* **4.** *in a large circle* **5.** Sentences will vary but each should tell how someone looked and sounded and one thing that person did.

© Macmillan/McGraw-Hill

Adding Details About People

Read each sentence. Add details about how people looked, sounded, and acted. Use the details from the box.

in a very loud voice	in a large circle
with purple feathers	did cartwheels

1. My aunt wore a hat _____ .

2. My brother _____ down the path.

3. Mr. Sands talked _____ .

4. Everyone gathered _____ .

Write two sentences. Describe a person. Include details about how this person looked, sounded, and acted. Use exact words.

5. _____

_____

_____

_____

_____

_____

_____

<u>WRITING STRATEGIES</u>

Adding Details About Things

TEACH/MODEL

Introduce the Writing Strategy   Remind children that adding details to an autobiographical narrative helps readers understand the story better. Say: *When you add details, think about what your readers might want to know about the things you saw, heard, smelled, tasted, or felt.*

- Write: *I have some fruit.* Point out how this sentence does not tell readers enough. Say: *I can add details about what I saw.* Write: *I have a yellow fuzzy peach.* Discuss other details a writer might add about what he or she saw.

- Say: *I can add details about what I heard.* Write: *I slurped the yellow fuzzy peach when I bit it.* Discuss other details about sounds that a writer might add.

- Say: *I can add details about what I smelled.* Write: *The yellow fuzzy peach smelled sweet.* Discuss other details about smells that a writer might add.

- Say: *I can add details about what I tasted.* Write: *The yellow fuzzy peach tasted sugary and tart.* Discuss other details about taste that a writer might add.

- Say: *I can add details about what I felt.* Write: *When I bit the yellow fuzzy peach I felt the juice dribble down my chin.* Discuss other details about touch or feel that a writer might add.

Reread each of the sentences you wrote. Point out how each detail you added created a clearer picture for readers.

Teach Using Exact Words   Say: *Exact words give readers a clearer picture of things that you saw, heard, smelled, tasted, or felt.* Write each sentence below. Have children rewrite each sentence, using one or more of the exact words. Discuss how the rewritten sentences paint clearer pictures.

Sentence Without Exact Words	Exact Words I Could Use
I saw <u>something</u>.	a dog; a plant; a boat
It felt <u>weird</u>.	soft; sticky; rough
It smelled <u>interesting</u>.	bitter; sweet; spicy

PRACTICE/APPLY

Practice Reproducible   Distribute **Practice Reproducible GW88.** Read the directions. Have individuals complete the exercises. Then ask partners to take turns reading aloud the details they wrote. Provide corrective feedback.

Answer Key: 1. *rough and scratchy* **2.** *a little sour* **3.** *dry brown* **4.** *whistling* **5.** *like peppermint* **6.** Sentences will vary but should use details to tell about a thing.

Adding Details About Things

Read each sentence. Add details about sight, sound, smell, taste, and touch. Use the details from the box.

like peppermint	dry brown
a little sour	rough and scratchy
whistling	

1. The new wool mittens felt _____
_____ .

2. The old milk tasted _____ .

3. The plant had _____ leaves.

4. A _____ noise came from
the kettle.

5. The candy smelled _____ .

Write two sentences. Describe a thing. Include details about what you saw, heard, smelled, tasted, or felt. Use exact words.

6. _____

_____

_____

_____

_____

Time Order

TEACH/MODEL

Introduce the Writing Strategy Explain that time order means a story is told in the order in which it happened, from what happened first to what happened last. Say: *Writing your autobiographical narrative in time order will keep your readers from being confused about what happened when.*

- Explain that it is important to decide when a story begins. Say: *First, decide when your story really begins. Then start the story with what happened first.*

- Say: *Then tell what happened next. Keep telling things in the correct time order until the very end.*

- Explain that writing in time order helps keep the writer and the writing organized. Say: *Time order will make your whole story clearer.*

Teach Using Time-Order Words Say: *Some words help you show time order. Words like* first, then, next, *and* finally *help tell what happened when.* Write the first paragraph below. Explain that starting each thought with a new sentence and a time-order word makes the story clearer. Include the time-order words below.

Without Time-Order Words	With Time-Order Words
Water gushed out of a pipe in the basement. We turned off the water. We called the plumber. He came and fixed the pipe!	Water gushed out of a pipe in the basement. <u>First</u>, we turned off the water. <u>Then</u> we called the plumber. <u>Finally</u>, he came and fixed the pipe!

PRACTICE/APPLY

Practice Reproducible Copy and distribute **Practice Reproducible GW89.** Read and discuss the directions. Then read together the sentences for children to reorder. Have individuals complete the exercises. Then ask partners to take turns reading one sentence each in correct order. Do partners agree on the order? Provide corrective feedback.

Answer Key: 1 *First, Mom took me to the animal shelter.* **2.** *Then I picked out two six-week-old kittens there.* **3.** *Next, we took them to the car.* **4.** *Finally, we brought them home.* **5.** Sentences will vary, but they should be in correct time order with time-order words.

Time Order

Read the events below. Then write them in time order below. Use time-order words from the box.

| first | next | then | finally |

We brought them home.

Mom took me to the animal shelter.

We took them to the car.

I picked out two six-week-old kittens there.

1. _____

2. _____

3. _____

4. _____

Write two or three sentences about something that happened to you. Tell everything in the correct time order. Use time-order words.

5. _____

_____

_____

_____

_____

WRITING STRATEGIES

Deleting Extra Details

TEACH/MODEL

Introduce the Writing Strategy Tell children that everything in their autobiographical narrative should relate to one event they are writing about. Explain that sometimes writers include extra details that don't really tell more about this one event. Say: *All the details you add should tell more about only this one event.*

Read Aloud a Model Read aloud this autobiographical narrative about someone breaking a cup. Say: *Some of the sentences do not belong because they tell about details not related to the topic.* Then model deleting extra details.

> Last summer, I visited my grandmother. She took me to a store to buy a present for my family. I knew I shouldn't touch anything in the store. My grandmother was born in Mexico. Then I saw a shelf of beautiful china cups. I picked one up, and it fell and broke.

- Ask: *What one event is this autobiographical narrative about?* (how the writer broke a cup in a store)

- Say: *When I read it over, I see a sentence that has nothing to do with dropping a cup in a store. The sentence* My grandmother was born in Mexico *has nothing to do with my story, even if the sentence itself is true.* Model crossing it out.

- Reread the autobiographical narrative, leaving out the sentence that doesn't belong. Discuss how now the story tells about only one event.

Teach Adding Details That Tell More Write each sentence below, one a time. Discuss whether each sentence tells more about the story you read above. Ask about each sentence: *Do these details help you understand what happened when the writer broke a cup? Why or why not?* Then invite children to suggest other sentences that could be added to tell more about the one event.

>   *My hands were slippery from eating buttered popcorn.* (yes; tells more)
>
>   *My brother plays baseball on Wednesdays.* (no; extra detail)

PRACTICE/APPLY

Practice Reproducible Distribute **Practice Reproducible GW90.** Read the directions. Then read the paragraphs together with children. Have individuals complete the exercises. Then ask partners to compare the sentences they crossed out. Did partners choose the same sentences to drop? Provide feedback.

Answer Key: 1. Extra Details: *My best friend was my cousin Billy. The next year my teacher was Mrs. Jacks.* **2.** Extra Details: *I live at 322 Main Street. Some candles have a nice smell.*

© Macmillan/McGraw-Hill

Deleting Extra Details

**Read these two autobiographical narratives.
There are two extra details in each one. Cross out
the extra details.**

1.   I used to go to a day care center. One warm
day, I went to the playground without my jacket.
At the end of the day, I couldn't find it. My best
friend was my cousin Billy. After everyone left, my
teacher found a jacket that wasn't mine. I wore it
home that night, although it was three sizes too big
for me. The next year my teacher was Mrs. Jacks.

2.   I live at 322 Main Street. When I was little, I
was afraid of storms. One night my parents went
out, and I was with a babysitter. She took out a
flashlight and candles. Some candles have a nice
smell. I knew there was going to be a storm. I
started to cry. The babysitter didn't know what to
do. Suddenly the phone rang. It was my parents.
After I talked to them, I felt fine.

<u>**WRITING APPLICATIONS**</u>

Prewriting an Autobiographical Narrative

TEACH/MODEL

Introduce the Writing Process   Say: *You can follow certain steps to make writing easier. These steps are called the writing process. They help you think of what to write and how to write it. I will show you how to follow these steps to write an autobiographical narrative.*

Introduce Prewriting   Explain that the first step of the writing process is **prewriting.** This is when writers think of what they want to say. Review what writers do during prewriting.

- Writers choose a topic. They decide what to write about.
- Writers brainstorm details. They think of many details that tell more about their topic. Then they write down words and phrases to help them remember the details.
- Writers organize details. They decide what happened first, second, third, and so on. They number their details in time order.

PRACTICE/APPLY

Practice Reproducible   Copy and distribute **Practice Reproducible GW91.** Read and discuss the directions and labels on the graphic organizer. Then pair each child with a partner. Provide the following support.

1. Help children choose a topic. Have children tell their topic to their partner. Say: *Think of something that happened to you this week or a long time ago. You could choose one of the events you wrote about on **Practice Reproducible GW85,** or you can think of something new.* Remind children that this should be something that happened to them.

2. Help them brainstorm details. Have children read the questions in the first box of the graphic organizer. Have them describe the beginning of their story to their partner before writing down details. Repeat with the middle and end. Prompt them as needed with questions such as these:

- *What happened first?*
- *What happened next?*
- *What details do you remember about an event, a place, people, or things?*
- *Are your details related to the event?*

3. Help them organize details. Ask: *Are your details in the right time order?* Have children number the details in the order they will write about them.

Prewriting an Autobiographical Narrative

Write about an event that happened to you. Tell what happened in the beginning, middle, and end. Add details in each box.

I remember when _____	
Beginning	What happened? Details about an event, a place, people, or things
Middle	What happened? Details about an event, a place, people, or things
End	What happened? Details about an event, a place, people, or things

Drafting an Autobiographical Narrative

TEACH/MODEL

Revisit Prewriting Help children review the graphic organizer they completed during prewriting: **Practice Reproducible GW91.** Have children reread what happened and the details they wrote. Tell them that they will use these to draft their autobiographical narrative.

Introduce Drafting Explain that the next step of the writing process is **drafting.** This is when writers reread their graphic organizers and turn their ideas into sentences. Review what writers do during drafting an autobiographical narrative.

- They write a beginning sentence. They write the first sentence that tells about the event they have chosen.

- They write sentences in time order. They use the details in their graphic organizer to tell the beginning, middle, and end of their story.

- They just write. They don't worry about mistakes. They will fix these later.

PRACTICE/APPLY

Practice Reproducible Copy and distribute **Practice Reproducible GW92.** Read and discuss the directions and the labels. Then have children work individually to complete it. Remind children to use the details they wrote on their prewriting graphic organizer. Provide the following support as children write.

1. Help children write a sentence about why the event is important to them. Ask questions such as these: *Why was the event special? What did you learn? Did you learn something about yourself? something about someone else?*

2. Help them write sentences to create a beginning, middle, and end. Write these sentence frames. Have children use or adapt the ones that fit their story.

Sentence Frames
When I was _____ years old, I _____ .
First, I _____ .
Then I _____ .
After that, _____ .
Finally, _____ .
I learned a lot about _____

Drafting an Autobiographical Narrative

Write one or two sentences in each box. Use the details you wrote during prewriting.

I Sentence About Why This Event Is
Important to Me

_____

_____

I-2 Sentences About the Beginning

_____

_____

I-2 Sentences About the Middle

_____

_____

I-2 Sentences About the End

_____

_____

WRITING APPLICATIONS

Revising an Autobiographical Narrative

TEACH/MODEL

Revisit Drafting Have children reread the sentences they drafted on **Practice Reproducible GW92.** Tell them that they will revise these sentences.

Introduce Revising Explain that the next step of the writing process is **revising.** This is when writers reread their writing and ask questions such as: *Are my sentences in the correct time order? Did I include enough details? Did I use exact words?* Explain that when writers revise, they often vary their sentences.

Teach Sentence Combining Explain that good writers vary the lengths of their sentences. They write some short sentences and some long sentences. Say: *One way to make a long sentence is to combine two shorter sentences using the word* or. Explain that the word *or* is used when the writer is talking about two choices.

- Write two short sentences: *We could go shopping today. We could go shopping tomorrow.* Combine them to write one longer sentence: *We could go shopping today or tomorrow.* Circle *or.* Discuss which words you included when you combined the sentence and which words you left out.

- Repeat with other examples. Write: *I might paint a picture. I might read a book.* Then write: *I might paint a picture or read a book.*

Teach Using Different Kinds of Sentences Explain that good writers vary the kinds of sentences they use. They might rewrite a statement as an exclamation.

- Write: *Mosquitoes are buzzing around.* Say: *This is a statement. It is one kind of sentence.* Circle the period.

- Then write: *That mosquito bit me!* Say: *This is an exclamation. This sentence shows strong feeling.* Circle the exclamation point. Explain that good writers don't use exclamations a lot. They save exclamations for very strong feelings.

PRACTICE/APPLY

Practice Reproducible Distribute **Practice Reproducible GW93.** Read the directions. Then have children work individually to complete the exercises. Provide corrective feedback. When children have finished, ask them to discuss with a partner the changes they made to their own papers.

Answer Key: 1. *I could meet you today or tomorrow.* **2.** *We could paint the bedroom or go to the movies.* **3.** Check to make sure children revise their papers. Answers will vary. **4.** Sample Answer: I saw a real elephant! **5.** Check to make sure children revise their papers. Answers will vary.

Revising an Autobiographical Narrative

Sentence Combining

Read each pair of short sentences. Rewrite them to make one longer sentence. Use *or*.

1. I could meet you today. I could meet you tomorrow.

_____

_____

2. We could paint the bedroom. We could go to the movies._____

_____

3. Now find two short sentences in your autobiographical narrative. Combine them to make one longer sentence using *or*.

Using Different Kinds of Sentences

Rewrite this sentence as an exclamation.

4. I saw an elephant.

_____

_____

5. Change one statement in your autobiographical narrative to an exclamation.

Assessment

TEACHER-STUDENT CONFERENCES

- If time allows, have a conference with each child about his or her writing.

- A few questions from an adult or a peer can clarify how to improve a piece of writing. Discussions can help young writers focus on audience and purpose.

- Have children read their paragraphs aloud to you. Listen attentively. Then prompt them to revise by asking questions such as those shown below.

- Try to start by identifying at least one or two things you like about the writing. Then focus on the content of what the child is trying to communicate.

- After your conference, help children decide how to revise their paragraphs.

Conference Questions

√ *What one event are you telling about? Do all your details focus on just this one topic?*

√ *You told some interesting details about _____ . What else happened when _____ ? What else did you see or hear? Who else was there?*

√ *The word _____ is not really clear. Is there another word you could use? What word says exactly what you mean?*

√ *What happened first? What happened second? Could you tell me more about that? Can you add any time-order words? Look back at the order words in the model on* **Practice Reproducible GW89.**

- Have children proofread their papers and make neat final copies.

USING THE RUBRIC

- Use the **Scoring Rubric.** Evaluate the child's writing one criterion at a time.

- You will often find that a child's writing receives different scores for different criteria. The final score, however, should be a single number. In reaching a holistic score, give the most weight to Genre and to Organization and Focus.

- Analyze each child's errors using the criteria and the lesson numbers provided. Reteach those lessons for skills that caused the child difficulty.

  Genre (Lessons 84–88; Lesson 92)
  Organization and Focus (Lessons 89–91)
  Sentence Structure (Lesson 93)
  Conventions (Lesson 93)

- Provide corrective feedback about errors in grammar, usage, and mechanics. If necessary, consider reteaching lessons in Sections 1–7.

Scoring Rubric

	Narrative Writing: Autobiographical
Score 4	**Genre** The writer tells about a single event and explains why the event was important. Details about people, places, or things help readers imagine what it was like to experience that event. Words are exact and interesting. **Organization and Focus** Events are told in time order, using order words. The writer includes only details that tell more about the important event. **Sentence Structure** The writer uses both long and short sentences as well as different kinds of sentences. **Conventions** There are not many mistakes in grammar, spelling, or punctuation.
Score 3	**Genre** The writer tells about a single event but may not explain why the event was important. The writer could tell more about people, places, or things. Some words could be more exact. **Organization and Focus** One or two events may be out of order. Order words may be missing. There may be some extra details. **Sentence Structure** Some of the sentences are short and choppy. The writer could vary sentences more. **Conventions** There are some mistakes but none make the writing hard to understand.
Score 2	**Genre** The writer does not tell about a single event. There are almost no details about people, places, or things. Many words are vague. **Organization and Focus** Many events are out of order. There are no sequence words. There are many extra details that do not tell more about the topic. **Sentence Structure** Many of the sentences are short and choppy. **Conventions** There are many mistakes. Some make the writing hard to understand.
Score 1	**Genre** The topic is not clear. There are no details. Words are vague or confusing. **Organization and Focus** There is no clear order. Most details are unrelated to the topic. **Sentence Structure** All the sentences are short and choppy. **Conventions** Mistakes make the writing hard to understand.

GENRE FEATURES

Fictional Narrative

TEACH/MODEL

Introduce the Genre   Discuss these features of fictional narrative.

- A **fictional narrative** is a story that you make up. It has a clear beginning, middle, and end. Say: *You can write a fictional narrative about a family going on a picnic or a class getting a pet.*

- **Events** are the things that happen in a fictional narrative. The events happen in an order that makes sense. Say: *If I wrote about a family picnic, I would tell the events in order.*

- The **setting** is the place where the events happen. It is also the time when these events happen. Say: *A family picnic could happen at lunchtime in a park.*

- The **characters** are the people in the fictional narrative. When the characters speak, their words are called **dialogue.**

- **Details** tell more about the setting, characters, objects, and events in a fictional narrative. Say: *I could include details about the park: The park had thick, green grass and a marble fountain. The water splashed loudly and birds chirped.*

Read Aloud a Model   Read this fictional narrative. Then discuss the questions.

> One morning at school, Mrs. Charles stood in her classroom. Twenty students sat at their desks. Mrs. Charles said, "Let's get a pet!"
> First, the children discussed classroom pets. Then they voted on which pet they would like to have. Finally, Mrs. Charles tallied the votes on the chalkboard. The hamster received the most votes. The next day, Mrs. Charles brought in a small tan hamster in a silver cage.

Discussion Questions   *What is the* **setting**? (morning at school) *Who are the* **characters**? (Mrs. Charles, students) *What is the* **dialogue** *in the story?* ("Let's get a pet!") *What happens in the* **beginning**? (talking about getting a class pet) *the* **middle**? (voting) *the* **end**? (bringing in hamster) *Which* **details** *describe the class pet?* (small, tan)

PRACTICE/APPLY

Practice Reproducible   Distribute **Practice Reproducible GW95.** Choral-read the model. Discuss each label. Ask partners to discuss the questions. Have them record their answers and then share them with the group. Provide feedback.

Answer Key: 1. Beginning: Liza skis down the mountain. **Middle:** Keith follows her. **End:** Keith meets Liza at the bottom. **2.** a ski slope at noon **3.** Liza and her brother Keith **4.** *"Here I go!"; "Wait for me!"; "Great job, Keith"* **5.** *the snow glinted like diamonds; the steep, icy mountain*

© Macmillan/McGraw-Hill

Fictional Narrative

**Read this fictional narrative. Study each label.
Then discuss the questions below with a partner.**

Character

Setting

Details

"Here I go!" called <u>Liza</u>. She whizzed down the <u>ski slope</u>, her <u>curly blond hair</u> streaming back. In the strong noon sun, the snow glinted like diamonds.

Setting

At the top of the steep, icy mountain, Liza's brother Keith struggled to point his skis downhill. "Wait for me!" ◄— Dialogue
Keith yelled.

As Liza watched from below, Keith started down. Keith skidded to a stop beside Liza, sending up a spray of snow. "Great job, Keith," said Liza.

1. What happens in the **beginning** of the story? In the **middle**? In the **end**?

2. What is the **setting**?

3. Who are the **characters**?

4. Find the **dialogue** in the story. Read it with a partner.

5. Which **details** describe the snow and the mountain? Read them to a partner.

WRITING STRATEGIES

Creating Characters

TEACH/MODEL

Introduce the Writing Strategy Remind children that a fictional narrative is a made-up story with a beginning, middle, and end. Say: *When you write a fictional narrative, you want readers to understand how a character looks and acts.*

- Write: *The girl went to the party.* Point out how this sentence does not tell readers enough. Ask: *What details can I add to describe what the girl looks like?*

- Say: *I can add details about what she looks like.* Write: *The <u>freckle-faced</u> girl went to the party.* Discuss other words a writer might add to tell what someone looks like.

- Say: *I can add details about clothing.* Write: *The freckle-faced girl in the <u>red dress</u> went to the party.* Discuss other words about clothing a writer might add.

- Say: *I can add details about actions.* Write: *The freckle-faced girl in the red dress <u>skipped</u> as she went to the party.* Discuss other action words a writer might add.

Point out how each detail you added created a clearer picture for readers.

Teach Using Exact Words Say: *Exact words give readers a clearer picture of how a character looks and acts.* Write each sentence below. Then brainstorm exact words to replace each underlined word. Start with the exact words listed below. Have children rewrite each sentence using one or more of these exact words. Discuss how the rewritten sentences give clearer pictures of the characters.

Sentence Without Exact Words	Exact Words I Could Use
The girl dried her <u>wet</u> hair.	soggy; damp; drenched; soaked
The <u>strong</u> man lifted the barbell.	powerful; muscular; brawny
The boy <u>laughed</u> at the joke.	chuckled; giggled; cackled; hooted

PRACTICE/APPLY

Practice Reproducible Distribute **Practice Reproducible GW96.** Read the directions. Then read together the sentences and the details in the box. Have individuals complete the exercises. Then ask partners to take turns reading aloud the descriptions they wrote of a character. Prompt each partner to ask the writer questions about how the character looks and acts. Provide feedback.

Answer Key: 1. *long-haired* **2.** *tiny, fussy* **3.** *swiftly and surely* **4.** *loudly and shrilly* **5.** Answers will vary.

Creating Characters

Read each sentence. Add details that tell how the character looks and acts. Use the details from the box.

tiny, fussy	loudly and shrilly
swiftly and surely	long-haired

1. The _____ man went to the barber.

2. The _____ baby cried in his crib.

3. The soccer player ran _____ toward the goal.

4. The gym teacher's whistle blew _____ .

Think of a character you have read about. Write two sentences. Include details that tell about how the character looks and acts. Use exact words.

5. _____

_____

_____

_____

_____

<u>**WRITING STRATEGIES**</u>

Adding Dialogue

TEACH/MODEL

Introduce the Writing Strategy   Remind children that a fictional narrative is a made-up story with a beginning, middle, and end. Say: *When you write a fictional narrative, you want readers to understand how a character talks.*

- Write: *The vet said the puppy was sick.* Point out how this sentence does not give enough details about the exact words that the vet speaks.

- Say: *I can add dialogue, or the exact words that the vet speaks.* Write: *The vet said, "This puppy has a bad cough and needs some medicine."* Discuss other dialogue a writer could add to show exactly what a vet might say.

- Point to the comma in the sentence. Say: *The comma separates the story words from the character's exact words.* Point to the quotation marks in the sentence. Say: *The quotation marks show the character's exact words.*

Teaching Using Exact Words for *Said*   Reread the sentence: *The vet said, "This puppy has a bad cough and needs some medicine."* Point to *said.* Say: *You can use other words in place of* said. Replace *said* with *stated, reported,* and *explained.* Discuss other words a writer might use for *said.* Write each sentence below. Then brainstorm words to replace *said.* Start with the words listed below. Have children rewrite each sentence using one or more of these words. Discuss how each rewritten sentence gives a clearer picture of how the character speaks.

Sentence With *Said*	Words to Replace *Said*
"Look out!" <u>said</u> the cab driver.	yelled; shouted; exclaimed; hollered
"Play this game," the teacher <u>said</u>.	suggested; offered; mentioned
Mom <u>said</u>, "This is a good map."	explained; declared; stated

PRACTICE/APPLY

Practice Reproducible   Copy and distribute **Practice Reproducible GW97.** Read and discuss the directions. Then read together the sentences and the dialogue in the box. Have individuals complete the exercises. Then ask partners to take turns reading aloud the dialogue they wrote. Prompt each partner to ask the writer questions about what the character said. Provide corrective feedback.

Answer Key: 1. *You need new tires.* **2.** *The soup is very good.* **3.** *Dad said, "We can take a train trip."* **4.** *"I live on Elm Street," explained the girl.* **5.** Answers will vary.

Adding Dialogue

Read each sentence. Add dialogue from the box for each character. Circle the comma and both quotation marks.

The soup is very good	You need new tires

1. The mechanic stated, " _____
_____ ."

2. The waiter suggested, " _____
_____ ."

Read each sentence. Add the missing commas and quotation marks.

3. Dad said We can take a train trip.

4. I live on Elm Street explained the girl.

Think of a character. Write two sentences of dialogue for the character. Use a comma and quotation marks.

5. _____
_____
_____
_____
_____
_____

<u>WRITING STRATEGIES</u>

Adding Details About Setting

TEACH/MODEL

Introduce the Writing Strategy   Remind children that a fictional narrative is a made-up story with a beginning, middle, and end. Review that the setting is the place where the events in the fictional narrative happen, as well as the time when these events happen. Say: *When you write a fictional narrative, you want to paint a picture of the setting for your readers.*

- Write: *Tom was at the ice rink.* Point out how this sentence does not tell readers enough. Ask: *What details can I add to describe the ice rink?*

- Say: *I can add details about what Tom sees at the ice rink.* Write: *A shabby wall enclosed the large oval ice rink.* Discuss other details a writer might add to describe how an ice rink looks.

- Say: *I can add details about what Tom hears at the ice rink.* Write: *The skaters' blades scraped on the ice.* Discuss other details to describe sounds at an ice rink.

- Say: *I can add details about what Tom smells at the ice rink.* Write: *The smell of popcorn drifted from a snack stand.* Discuss other smell details to add.

- Say: *I can add details about what Tom feels at the ice rink.* Write: *The air felt icy cold.* Discuss other details a writer might add about how an ice rink feels.

Point out how each detail you added paints a clearer picture for readers.

Teach Using Exact Words   Say: *Exact words give readers a clearer picture of what a setting is like.* Write these sentences. Then brainstorm exact words to replace each underlined word. Have children rewrite each sentence using these exact words. Discuss how the rewritten sentences paint a clearer picture of the setting.

Sentence Without Exact Words	Exact Words I Could Use
The library is <u>quiet</u>.	silent; hushed; still
We went to a <u>big</u> house.	gigantic; huge; enormous
The garden had a <u>nice</u> smell.	sweet; fragrant; perfumed

PRACTICE/APPLY

Practice Reproducible   Distribute **Practice Reproducible GW98.** Read the directions. Have individuals complete the exercises. Have partners take turns reading the descriptions they wrote of a place. Prompt each partner to ask the writer questions about how the place looks, sounds, smells, feels, and tastes.

 Answer Key: 1. *and burns your face* **2.** *dusty, golden* **3.** *howling and yipping* **4.** *of heavy smoke* **5.** Answers will vary.

Adding Details About Setting

Read each sentence. Add details that tell what you might see, hear, smell, and feel. Use the details from the box.

dusty, golden	and burns your face
of heavy smoke	howling and yipping

1. The sun shines _____
   in the desert.

2. The _____ sand stretches for miles.

3. We heard a coyote _____
   in the distance.

4. The wind carries a smell _____
   _____ .

Describe a place you know. Write two sentences. Include details that tell what you might see, hear, smell, feel, and taste in that place. Use exact words.

5. _____

   _____

   _____

   _____

   _____

Beginning, Middle, End

TEACH/MODEL

Introduce the Writing Strategy Remind children that a fictional narrative is a made-up story with a beginning, middle, and end. Say: *When you write a fictional narrative, you need to start with an idea. Then think about the order in which you tell the events so readers can understand what is happening.*

- Say: *To get started writing a fictional narrative, I ask myself "What if?" questions. What if a girl joined a band? What if a class wrote letters to pen pals?*

- Work with children to brainstorm other story ideas, using the question "What if?" Record children's ideas in a list like the one shown below.

What if _____ **?**

a family planted a vegetable garden

the school bus broke down

a class visited an aquarium

a storm knocked out the power

Beginning, Middle, End Say: *A clear beginning, middle, and end help readers understand what is happening in a story. My story idea is:* What if a class wrote letters to pen pals?

- Write: *Mrs. Getz told the class they would write to pen pals. They would send their letters to a class in Ireland.* Say: *This is the beginning of the story. It includes the detail that the pen pals are in Ireland.*

- Write: *The students wrote letters. They wrote about books they were reading and about planting bean seeds. Mrs. Getz mailed the letters.* Say: *This is the middle of the story. It includes details about what the students wrote in their letters.*

- Write: *Three weeks later, Mrs. Getz had a surprise for the class. Eighteen letters had arrived from Ireland!* Say: *This is the end of the story. It includes details about when and how many letters arrived.*

PRACTICE/APPLY

Practice Reproducible Copy and distribute **Practice Reproducible GW99.** Read and discuss the directions. Have individuals complete the exercises. Then ask partners to share what they wrote for the beginning, middle, and end of one story. Prompt each partner to ask about details in each part of the story. Provide corrective feedback.

Answer Key: Answers will vary but should show that the children are thinking about the beginning, middle, and end of two different story ideas.

Beginning, Middle, End

Complete each "What if?" question. Write what might happen in the beginning, middle, and end of each story. Include details for each part of each story.

What if _____ **?**
What might happen in the beginning?
What might happen in the middle?
What might happen in the end?

What if _____ **?**
What might happen in the beginning?
What might happen in the middle?
What might happen in the end?

Prewriting a Fictional Narrative

TEACH/MODEL

Introduce the Writing Process   Say: *You can follow certain steps to make writing easier. These steps are called the writing process. They help you think of what to write and how to write it. I will show you how to follow these steps to write a fictional narrative.*

Introduce Prewriting   Explain that the first step of the writing process is **prewriting.** This is when writers think of what they want to say. Review what writers do during prewriting.

- Writers choose a story idea. They decide what to write about.
- Writers brainstorm events. They write down words and phrases to help them remember the events.
- Writers organize events. They think about what might happen in the beginning, middle, and end of the story. They list the events in order.
- Writers brainstorm details. They think of many details that tell more about the setting, characters, objects, and events. Then they write down words and phrases to help them remember the details.

PRACTICE/APPLY

Practice Reproducible   Distribute **Practice Reproducible GW100.** Read the directions and the labels. Pair each child with a partner. Provide this support.

1. Help them choose a story idea. Tell children they can pick one of the story ideas from **Practice Reproducible GW99.** Have them tell their ideas to their partners. Ask: *Can you think of a clear beginning, middle, and end? Can you describe the setting using some of your five senses? Can you describe how the characters look, act, and talk?*

2. Help them brainstorm events and details. Have children read each label on the graphic organizer. Tell them to describe to their partner what might happen in the beginning, middle, and end of the story before writing down any words or phrases. Prompt children as needed with questions such as these:

- Beginning *What is the setting? How does the place look, sound, smell, feel, taste? Who are the characters? How do they look, act, and talk? What are the first events?*
- Middle *What events happen in the middle of the story? What details can you add about the characters, dialogue, or setting?*
- End *How does the story end? What details can you add about the characters, dialogue, or setting?*

3. Help them organize events. Ask: *Do the events happen in an order that makes sense? Can a reader follow the story from beginning to end?*

Prewriting a Fictional Narrative

Complete the "What if?" question. Write what might happen in the beginning, middle, and end of the story. Include details for each part of the story.

What if	_____ ?
Beginning	What might happen? Add details about characters, dialogue, or setting.
Middle	What might happen? Add details about characters, dialogue, or setting.
End	What might happen? Add details about characters, dialogue, or setting.

Drafting a Fictional Narrative

TEACH/MODEL

Revisit Prewriting Help children review the graphic organizer they completed during prewriting: **Practice Reproducible GW100.** Have them reread events and details. Tell them that they will use these to draft their fictional narratives.

Introduce Drafting Explain that the next step of the writing process is **drafting.** This is when writers turn their events and details into sentences. Review what writers do when they draft a fictional narrative.

- They write sentences about what happens in the beginning, middle, and end of the story. They use the details in their graphic organizer to write sentences that tell more about the events, as well as the character, dialogue, and setting.

- They write dialogue for the characters.

- They just write. They don't worry about mistakes. They will fix these later.

PRACTICE/APPLY

Practice Reproducible Distribute **Practice Reproducible GW101.** Read and discuss the directions and the labels on the graphic organizer. Have children work individually to complete it. Remind them to use the events and details they wrote on their prewriting graphic organizer. Provide the following support.

1. Help them write a sentence to answer "What if?" Ask questions such as: *What story are you telling? How can you describe your story idea in one sentence?*

2. Help them write sentences for the beginning, middle, and end. Ask questions: *How can you describe what happens in the beginning in one sentence? What details can you include about the setting, characters, objects, and events?*

3. Help them write dialogue and use time-order words. Write these sentence frames. Prompt children to use or adapt the ones that fit their dialogue and events. Point out time-order words such as *First* and *Then*. Ask: *What do the characters say? What time-order words can you use to show the order of events?*

Sentence Frames
He said, " _____ ."
" _____ ," she shouted.
First, _____ .
Then _____ .
Next, _____ .
Finally, _____ .

Drafting a Fictional Narrative

Write one sentence about your "What if?" question.
Write one or two sentences to tell what happens in
the beginning, middle, and end of the story. Include
details. Use the details you wrote during prewriting.

My "What If?" Question
_____

Beginning
_____
_____
_____

Middle
_____
_____
_____

End
_____
_____
_____

Revising a Fictional Narrative

TEACH/MODEL

Revisit Drafting   Have children reread the sentences they drafted on **Practice Reproducible GW101.** Tell them that they will revise these sentences to make them better.

Introduce Revising   Explain that the next step of the writing process is **revising.** This is when writers reread their writing and ask themselves questions such as these: *Did I write sentences about the beginning, middle, and end of the story? Did I include enough details? Did I use exact words?* Explain that when they revise, writers often vary their sentences.

Teach Sentence Combining   Explain that good writers vary the length of their sentences. They write some short sentences and some long sentences. Say: *One way to make a long sentence is to combine two shorter sentences using* because.

- Write two short sentences: *The kitten meowed. The kitten was hungry.* Combine them to write one longer sentence: *The kitten meowed because it was hungry.* Circle *because.* Discuss what words you included when you combined the sentence and what words you changed.

- Repeat with other examples. Write: *The ground is wet. It rained.* Then write: *The ground is wet because it rained.*

Teach Using Different Kinds of Sentences   Explain that good writers also vary the kinds of sentences they use. They might rewrite a statement as a command.

- Write: *The dog needs a bath.* Say: *This is a declarative sentence. It tells about someone or something.* Circle the word *needs.*

- Then write: *Give the dog a bath.* Say: *This is an imperative sentence. This kind of sentence tells someone what to do.* Circle the word *Give.*

- Repeat with other examples. Write: *Running in the school halls is not allowed.* Then write: *Don't run in the school halls.*

PRACTICE/APPLY

Practice Reproducible   Distribute **Practice Reproducible GW102.** Read the directions. Then have children work individually to complete the exercises. Circulate around the room. Provide feedback. When children have finished, ask them to discuss with a partner the changes they made to their own papers.

Answer Key: 1. The girl takes a nap because she is tired. 2. Dad washes the car because it is dirty. **3.** Check to make sure children revise their papers. Answers will vary. **4.** Sample Answer: Shut off the computer. **5.** Check to make sure children revise their papers. Answers will vary.

© Macmillan/McGraw-Hill

Revising a Fictional Narrative

Sentences Combining

Read each pair of short sentences. Rewrite them to make one longer sentence. Use *because*.

1. The girl takes a nap. The girl is tired.

_____

_____

2. Dad washes the car. The car is dirty.

_____

_____

3. Now find two short sentences in your fictional narrative. Combine them to make one longer sentence using *because*.

Using Different Kinds of Sentences

Read this declarative sentence. Then rewrite it. Make it an imperative sentence that tells someone what to do.

4. The computer should be shut off.

_____

5. Change one statement in your fictional narrative to a command.

Assessment

TEACHER-STUDENT CONFERENCES

- If time allows, have a conference with each child about his or her writing.

- A few questions from an adult or a peer can clarify how to improve a piece of writing. Discussions can help young writers focus on audience and purpose.

- Have children read their paragraphs aloud to you. Listen attentively. Then prompt them to revise by asking questions such as those shown below.

- Try to start by identifying at least one or two things you like about the writing. Then focus on the content of what the child is trying to communicate.

- After your conference, help them decide how to revise their paragraphs.

Conference Questions

√ *Can you tell me more about this story? What happens first? What happens in the middle? What happens at the end?*

√ *I want to know more about the character _____ . What does this character look like? How does he or she talk and act?*

√ *I want to know more about where all this happens. What would someone see there? What would the person hear or feel?*

√ *The word _____ is not really clear. Is there another word you could use? What word says exactly what you mean?*

√ *Did you use any dialogue? Did you use quotation marks with your dialogue? Look back at the model on* **Practice Reproducible GW95.**

- Have children proofread their papers and make neat final copies.

USING THE RUBRIC

- Use the **Scoring Rubric.** Evaluate the child's writing one criterion at a time.

- You will often find that a child's writing receives different scores for different criteria. The final score, however, should be a single number. In reaching a holistic score, give the most weight to Genre and to Organization and Focus.

- Analyze each child's errors, using the criteria and the lesson numbers provided. Reteach those lessons for skills that caused the child difficulty.

     Genre (Lessons 95–99; Lesson 102)

     Organization and Focus (Lessons 100–101)

     Sentence Structure (Lesson 102)

- Provide corrective feedback about errors in grammar, usage, and mechanics. If necessary, consider reteaching lessons in Sections 1–7.

Scoring Rubric

	Narrative Writing: Fictional
Score 4	**Genre** The writer tells a fictional story with a clear beginning, middle, and end. Details tell more about setting, characters, objects, and events. Words are exact and interesting. **Organization and Focus** Events are told in time order, using time-order words. The writer includes only details that help readers understand the story. **Sentence Structure** The writer uses both long and short sentences as well as different kinds of sentences. **Conventions** There are not many mistakes in grammar, spelling, or punctuation.
Score 3	**Genre** The writer tells a fictional story with a beginning, middle, and end. There may not be many details about setting, characters, objects, and events. Some words could be more exact. **Organization and Focus** One or two events may be out of order. Time-order words may be missing. There may be some extra details. **Sentence Structure** Some of the sentences are short and choppy. The writer could vary sentences more. **Conventions** There are some mistakes but none make the writing hard to understand.
Score 2	**Genre** The beginning, middle, or end may be missing or unclear. There are almost no details about setting, characters, objects, and events. Many words are vague. **Organization and Focus** Many events are out of order. There are no time-order words. There are many extra details that do not tell more about the topic. **Sentence Structure** Many of the sentences are short and choppy. **Conventions** There are many mistakes. Some make the writing hard to understand.
Score 1	**Genre** The topic is not clear. There are no details. Words are vague or confusing. **Organization and Focus** There is no clear order. Most details are unrelated to the topic. **Sentence Structure** All the sentences are short and choppy. **Conventions** Mistakes make the writing hard to understand.

<u>**GENRE FEATURES**</u>

Informational Paragraph

TEACH/MODEL

Introduce the Genre Discuss these features of an informational paragraph while reviewing and reinforcing academic language.

- An **informational paragraph** is a group of sentences with facts about a topic that the audience may not know much about. Authors write informational paragraphs to inform readers. Say: *You can write an informational paragraph about something you have read, a person, an animal or thing, a special event, or a place.*

- You write about only one **topic** or subject in an informational paragraph. Say: *If you tell facts about the life of a bat from a book, then the life of a bat is your topic.*

- You begin with a clear **topic sentence** that tells readers what the paragraph is about. Because the topic sentence comes first in the paragraph, it is indented.

- You write **supporting sentences** that tell your readers important **facts** and **information** about the topic. Say: *If your topic is the life of a bat, you might write about what a bat eats or how a bat sleeps.*

- You write **exact words** to make the information clear and interesting. Say: *You might write* bats use thin wings made of skin to fly, *instead of* bats can fly.

Read Aloud a Model Read the informational paragraph. Discuss the questions.

> Our sailboat is beautiful and lots of fun, too. It is seventy years old and made of wood. It has a tall spruce mast and one white sail with the number 15 on it. The sides of the boat are white with a long green stripe at the top. The name of our sailboat is *Jessica*, and we sail in it in the spring and summer. On warm, breezy days, we put on our life jackets and climb into *Jessica* for an exciting sailboat ride around Mystic Harbor.

- *Which sentence is the **topic sentence** of this informational paragraph?*
- *Which **supporting sentence** tells the age of the sailboat?*
- *What **facts** and **information** did you learn about the sailboat?*
- *Which **exact words** describe the days on which the family goes sailing?*

PRACTICE/APPLY

Practice Reproducible Copy and distribute **Practice Reproducible GW104.** Choral-read the model. Point out the indented line and discuss labels. Ask partners to discuss the questions, then record and share answers. Provide feedback.

Answer Key: 1. *Fish* **2.** *easy to care for, you can buy them in most pet shops* **3.** *Did you know that fish come in all sizes and colors? Some are huge and colorful, but others are tiny and almost clear.* **4.** *clear, fresh, a few flakes; terrific, huge, colorful, tiny*

Informational Paragraph

Read this informational paragraph. Study each label. Then answer the questions below.

Topic Sentence   Facts and information

Topic → <u>Fish</u> make terrific pets! They are <u>easy to care for</u>, and <u>you can buy them in most pet shops</u>. Did you know that fish come in all sizes and colors? Some are huge and colorful, but others are tiny and almost clear. Many people keep goldfish as pets. Their scales are gold, and they are ← Supporting Sentence
about as big as your thumb. All that most fish need to live is a <u>clear</u> bowl, <u>fresh</u> water, and <u>a few flakes</u> of food ← Exact Words
each day.

1. Find the **topic sentence** in this informational paragraph. Read it to your partner. What is the **topic**?

2. Read the first **supporting sentence** to your partner. What facts and information does he or she hear in it?

3. Which **supporting sentences** tell about the sizes and colors of fish? Read one to your partner and have him or her read another to you.

4. Find the **exact words** used in the last supporting sentence. Read them to your partner. Together, find three other exact words in the paragraph.

<u>**WRITING STRATEGIES**</u>

Taking Notes

TEACH/MODEL

Introduce the Writing Strategy   Say: *Before you write an informational paragraph, you need to know enough about your topic to make the paragraph interesting for your readers. To make sure you have enough facts and information about your topic, follow these steps:*

1. List what you know about your topic. Then think about other facts and information that your audience might like to know about it.

2. Write down two or three questions that ask about your topic.

3. Read a book or a magazine that tells about your topic. As you read, look for facts that answer the questions.

4. Write answers to the questions.

Teach Taking Notes   Say: *When you write facts that answer the questions, do not copy entire sentences from what you've read. Instead, write answers quickly as notes.* **Notes** *are single words or phrases to remind you of the facts and answers you found.*

• Draw a note card like Note Card 1 below. Model asking the question. Then read the paragraph on page 211. (You will distribute the page later.) After finding the answer, model writing it in note form on the card. Call attention to the informality and brevity of your notes and how quickly you jot them down.

• Repeat the process with Note Card 2, having an individual read the question and then the paragraph to answer it. Assist the child as he or she rereads the sentence that has the answer and then rewrites it in note form.

Note Card 1	Note Card 2
Question: How is a bat like a bird?	**Question:** Do bats have feathers like birds do?
Notes: <u>has wings; can fly</u>	**Notes:** <u>no; hair or fur on body</u>

PRACTICE/APPLY

Practice Reproducible   Copy and distribute **Practice Reproducible GW105.** Read and discuss the directions. Together, read the informational paragraph. Have individuals reread to answer each question and then record the answer in note form below it. Have partners share and compare their notes. Provide feedback.

Answer Key: 1. *fruit, pollen, fish, insects* **2.** *caves, trees, tunnels, bridges, bat houses*

© Macmillan/McGraw-Hill

Taking Notes

Read the question on each note card. Then reread the informational paragraph about bats below. Write notes on each card to answer the question.

Bats

Bats are strange creatures. They use their wings to fly, but they are not birds. Bats are mammals that look like flying mice. They have hair or fur on their bodies. When bats sleep, they hang upside down. Some bats live in caves, trees, tunnels, or under bridges. Others live in bat houses that humans buy or build for them. Did you know that some bats eat fruit, pollen, and small fish? Others eat lots of insects, and that is why people provide homes for bats in their yards.

Note Card 1
Question: What do bats eat?
Notes: _____
_____

Note Card 2
Question: Where do bats live?
Notes: _____
_____

WRITING STRATEGIES

Planning Topic Sentences

TEACH/MODEL

Introduce the Writing Strategy   Say: *We have learned that the topic of an informational paragraph is the person, animal, place, thing, or event that the author is writing about. We have also learned that by asking questions, reading, and taking notes, we can get more facts and information about a topic.* Then explain that once enough facts have been collected, the writer needs to think about and organize them.

Teach Planning Topic Sentences   List these facts on the board and read them aloud: *growl loudly; throw food; huge sharp teeth; make faces at people; long pointed claws; chase other monkeys.* Explain that the facts are about two different topics: monkeys and tigers. Using a chart like the one below, model categorizing one of the facts and writing it under the correct topic. Have children assist you in categorizing each of the remaining facts. Then discuss the facts in each column and model writing a topic sentence that reflects them.

Facts About Monkeys	Facts About Tigers
throw food	long pointed claws
make faces at people	huge sharp teeth
chase other monkeys	growl loudly
Topic Sentence: Monkeys are very funny.	**Topic Sentence:** Tigers look and sound scary.

PRACTICE/APPLY

Practice Reproducible   Copy and distribute **Practice Reproducible GW106.** Read aloud and discuss the directions. Together, read aloud the list of facts in the box and the two topic sentences in the chart. Then have individuals categorize each fact under the correct topic sentence. Ask children to share their work with a partner and explain why they categorized the facts as they did. Provide corrective feedback.

Answer Key: **1.** *2 inches long; smallest birds in world; weigh half an ounce* **2.** *more than 8 feet tall; can weigh 1,000 pounds; largest meat-eating animal on land*

© Macmillan/McGraw-Hill

Planning Topic Sentences

Read the facts in the box. Then read the two topic sentences on the chart. Write each fact under the correct topic sentence.

- 2 inches long
- more than 8 feet tall
- smallest birds in the world
- can weigh 1,000 pounds
- weigh half an ounce
- largest meat-eating animal on land

1	2
Topic Sentence: Bee hummingbirds are tiny.	**Topic Sentence:** Polar bears are huge.
_____ _____	_____ _____
_____ _____	_____ _____
_____ _____	_____ _____

WRITING STRATEGIES

Writing Topic Sentences

TEACH/MODEL

Introduce the Writing Strategy Say: *We have learned that a* **topic sentence** *begins an informational paragraph. It is the first sentence that the audience reads, so it must be very clear and precise.* Then explain these functions of a topic sentence:

- A topic sentence tells the reader what the topic or subject is. It identifies what the paragraph will be about. Say: *If your topic is robots, then the word* robots *should be in your topic sentence.*

- A topic sentence also gives the reader a hint about the kind of facts and information they will read in the paragraph. Say: *If the facts and information you have collected tell only about the amazing things that robots can do, then you must state that in your topic sentence. For example, you might write:* Robots are able to do many amazing things.

Teach Writing a Topic Sentence Display a chart like the one below, omitting the topic sentence in the first row. Then read aloud the chart's contents. Tell children that the facts are about one topic, cars. Then say: *I see that all of the facts name errands or activities that cars are used for. Their usefulness is something that I'll want to mention when I write my topic sentence.* Model writing a topic sentence such as the one in the chart. Reinforce that the sentence names the topic and gives readers a hint about the kind of facts they will read about cars. Then have children suggest other topic sentences that could replace the one you wrote.

Topic Sentence: Cars are very useful.
Facts About Cars
used for grocery shopping
used to take kids to school, doctor, dentist, sports, music lessons
used by parents to get to and from work

PRACTICE/APPLY

Practice Reproducible Copy and distribute **Practice Reproducible GW107.** Read aloud and discuss the directions. Together, read aloud the topic and list of facts in each box. Have individuals complete the sentence frame in each box to write a topic sentence. Then have partners share their work. Provide corrective feedback.

Answer Key: 1. *Teachers are very helpful.* **2.** *Flags come in many sizes and shapes.*

Writing Topic Sentences

Read the topic and the facts in each box. Think carefully about them. Then complete the topic sentence at the top of each box.

Topic Sentence: _____ are very
_____ .

Facts About Teachers

help students learn to read and write

help children who don't feel well

help children find lost lunches and jackets

Topic Sentence: _____ come in
many _____ and _____ .

Facts About Flags

some are the size of a blanket; others are as huge as a trailer truck

some are small enough to hold and wave

some are shaped like a rectangle; others like a square or a triangle

WRITING STRATEGIES

Writing Supporting Sentences

TEACH/MODEL

Introduce the Writing Strategy   Say: *We know that an informational paragraph contains two kinds of sentences. One is the topic sentence. It names the topic and gives readers a hint about the kind of facts they will be reading. The other is supporting sentences that the author writes using facts and information that he or she has listed about the topic.* Explain these characteristics of supporting sentences:

- Supporting sentences tell important information about the topic in the topic sentence and do not contain information about other topics. Say: *If your topic is playing soccer, you would not have a supporting sentence about playing checkers.*

- Supporting sentences contain the kinds of facts and information that are hinted at in the topic sentence. Say: *If your topic sentence is* Lakes are beautiful places, *you would not include facts about an ugly lake in a supporting sentence.*

Teach Writing a Supporting Sentence   Display the chart below, omitting the supporting sentences. Read aloud the topic, the topic sentence, and the facts. Draw a line through the second fact, explaining that it has nothing to do with a tree. Model using the other facts to write the supporting sentences on the chart.

Topic: a big tree	
Topic Sentence: A big tree provides lots of fun for kids.	
Facts	**Supporting Sentences**
can play in tree house	Playing with friends in a tree house is exciting and enjoyable.
fun to hide behind big rocks	
can roll and hide in piles of leaves	It is great fun to roll and hide in huge piles of tree leaves.

PRACTICE/APPLY

Practice Reproducible   Copy and distribute **Practice Reproducible GW108.** Read and discuss the directions, facts, and topic sentence. Have individuals delete the irrelevant facts and write two supporting sentences using the remaining facts. Have partners share and work together to improve sentences. Provide feedback.

Answer Key: 1. Cross out: *scooters—small and quick* and *also need a helmet with inline skates* **2.** Sample Sentences: Racing bikes are light and very fast. They have thin tires. Mountain bikes are strong and sturdy. They have thick tires.

© Macmillan/McGraw-Hill

Writing Supporting Sentences

Complete each exercise.

1. Read the facts in the box. Think carefully about
them. Draw a line through the two facts that do
not belong with the others.

Facts About Bikes
racing bikes—light and very fast with thin tires
scooters—small and quick
mountain bikes—strong and sturdy with thick tires
also need a helmet with inline skates

2. Read the topic sentence below. Then reread the
Facts About Bikes that you did not cross out. Use
these facts to write two supporting sentences.

There are many different kinds of bikes. _____

_____

_____

_____

_____

_____

Prewriting an Informational Paragraph

TEACH/MODEL

Introduce the Writing Process   Say: *You can follow certain steps to make writing easier. These steps are called the writing process. They help you think of what to write and how to write it. I will help you follow these steps to write an informational paragraph.*

Introduce Prewriting   Explain that the first step of the writing process is **prewriting.** This is when writers think about their topic and the facts they will share with their readers. Review what writers do during prewriting.

• Writers choose a topic. They choose a subject that they know about and that their readers might like to learn about.

• Writers recall what they know about their topic and then ask a question about it. Sometimes, they read to find facts that answer their question. Then they write the facts in the form of words and short phrases.

• Writers organize their facts. They decide which facts their readers will want to read about first, second, third, and so on. They number facts in that order.

PRACTICE/APPLY

Practice Reproducible   Copy and distribute **Practice Reproducible GW109.** Read aloud and discuss the directions and the labels on the graphic organizer. Then pair each child with a partner. Provide the following support.

1. Help children choose a topic. Suggest that children write about an animal, place, thing, or event that they are familiar with. Have them list several topics and choose one. Ask: *Have you chosen a topic that you know enough about? Will your readers enjoy reading and learning about it?*

2. Help children write a question about their topic. Then have children share and discuss the question with their partners. Ask: *Will you be able to list facts to answer this question?*

3. Help children brainstorm facts. Have them think of facts they know that answer their question. Encourage them to discuss their facts with their partners before writing them. Prompt them as needed with questions such as these:

• *Does each fact answer the question you wrote?*

• *Will your audience find each fact interesting?*

• *Do you have enough interesting facts to write a paragraph?*

4. Help children organize their facts. Ask: *Which fact will you write about first? second? third?* Have them number facts in the order they will write about them.

Prewriting an Informational Paragraph

Write your topic. Then write a question about it. Write facts that answer the question in the boxes. Number the facts in the order you will write about them.

My Topic _____

My Question _____

_____

Fact	Fact	Fact
_____	_____	_____
_____	_____	_____
_____	_____	_____
_____	_____	_____
_____	_____	_____
_____	_____	_____
_____	_____	_____

_____ _____ _____

WRITING APPLICATIONS

Drafting an Informational Paragraph

TEACH/MODEL

Revisit Prewriting Help children review the graphic organizer they completed during prewriting: **Practice Reproducible GW109.** Have them reread their facts. Tell them that they will use these facts to write an informational paragraph.

Introduce Drafting Explain that the next step of the writing process is **drafting.** This is when writers reread their graphic organizers and turn their facts into sentences. Review what writers do during drafting.

• They write a topic sentence. They write one sentence that names their topic and gives a hint about the kind of facts that will be in their paragraph.

• They write supporting sentences in the order in which they numbered their facts on their graphic organizer.

• They just write. They don't worry about mistakes. They will fix these later.

PRACTICE/APPLY

Practice Reproducible Copy and distribute **Practice Reproducible GW110.** Read the directions and have children individually complete it. Remind children to use facts on their prewriting graphic organizer. Provide the following support.

1. Help children write a topic sentence. Ask: *What is your topic? Did you name this animal, place, thing, or event in the topic sentence? Does your topic sentence give a hint about the kinds of facts that you will put in your paragraph?*

2. Help children write supporting sentences. Assist as children write sentences that include facts from their graphic organizer. Reinforce that they should write supporting sentences in the same order that they numbered their facts. Write the sentence frames below. Prompt children to use or adapt the ones that fit the facts they will include or to think of other appropriate frames with a partner.

Sentence Frames

_____ are _____ .

A _____ is _____ .

I saw _____ .

I heard _____ .

They _____ .

It was _____ .

© Macmillan/McGraw-Hill

Drafting an Informational Paragraph

Look at the topic and facts on your prewriting graphic organizer. Below, write a topic sentence about the event. Then write three supporting sentences.

Topic Sentence

_____

_____

Supporting Sentence #1

_____

_____

Supporting Sentence #2

_____

_____

Supporting Sentence #3

_____

_____

WRITING APPLICATIONS

Revising an Informational Paragraph

TEACH/MODEL

Revisit Prewriting   Have children reread the sentences they drafted on **Practice Reproducible GW110.** Tell them that they will revise these sentences to make them better.

Introduce Revising   Explain that the next step of the writing process is **revising.** This is when writers reread their sentences and ask themselves questions such as these: *Did I write a clear, precise topic sentence? Did I write supporting sentences that tell more about this topic sentence? Did I use exact words?*

Teach Sentence Combining   Explain that good writers vary the lengths of their sentences. They write some short sentences and some long ones. Say: *One way to make a long sentence is to combine two shorter sentences using* and, but, *or* or.

- Write two short sentences: *The play began at seven o'clock. The play ended at nine.* Combine them to write one longer sentence: *The play began at seven o'clock and ended at nine.* Circle *and.* Discuss which words you included when you combined the sentences and which words you left out.

- Repeat with other examples. Write: *Jen had a cold. She still sang well.* Then write: *Jen had a cold but still sang well.* Write: *I didn't know if I should clap. I didn't know if I should cheer.* Then write: *I didn't know if I should clap or cheer.*

Teach Using Exact Words   Explain that good writers choose the words they use very carefully. When they revise, good writers replace weak or vague words with others that are strong and tell exactly what they mean.

- Write: *The play was good.* Say: *In this sentence,* good *is a weak word. The writer could replace it with a stronger, more exact word like* wonderful *or* fantastic.

- Then write: *The actor spoke loudly.* Say: *The writer could replace* spoke loudly *with the exact word* shouted. Write this revised sentence: *The actor shouted.*

PRACTICE/APPLY

Practice Reproducible   Copy and distribute **Practice Reproducible GW111.** Read and discuss the directions and the exercises. Then have children work individually to complete them. Circulate and provide corrective feedback. When children have finished, have them discuss with a partner the changes they made.

Answer Key: 1. The costumes were fancy and looked realistic. **2.** The dancers leaped across the stage but never fell down. **3.** Answers will vary. **4.** Sample answer: The actor *tiptoed* toward the audience and *whispered* his lines. **5.** Answers will vary.

Revising an Informational Paragraph

Sentence Combining

Read each pair of short sentences. Rewrite them to make one longer sentence. Use *and* in sentence I and *but* in sentence 2.

1. The costumes were fancy. They looked realistic.

_____

_____

2. The dancers leaped across the stage. They never fell down. _____

_____

3. Now, find two short sentences in your informational paragraph. Combine them to write one longer sentence using *and* or *but*.

Using Exact Words

Replace each underlined word with an exact word. Then write the revised sentence

4. The actor <u>moved</u> toward the audience and <u>said</u> his lines. _____

_____

5. Now replace two words in your paragraph with two exact words.

Assessment

TEACHER-STUDENT CONFERENCES

- If time allows, have a conference with each child about his or her writing.

- A few questions from an adult or a peer can clarify how to improve a piece of writing. Discussions can help young writers focus on audience and purpose.

- Have children read their paragraphs aloud to you. Listen attentively. Then prompt them to revise by asking questions such as those shown below.

- Try to start by identifying at least one or two things you like about the writing. Then focus on the content of what the child is trying to communicate.

- After your conference, help them decide how to revise their paragraphs.

Conference Questions

√ *What topic are you telling me about? Do all your facts tell about just this one topic?*

√ *You told me some interesting facts about _____ . What else did you learn about this?*

√ *The word _____ is not really clear. Is there another word you could use? What word says exactly what you mean?*

√ *When you first started reading, I wasn't sure what topic you were writing about. Can you make that clear in the first sentence? Look back at the topic sentence in the model on* **Practice Reproducible GW104.**

- Have children proofread their papers and make neat final copies.

USING THE RUBRIC

- Use the **Scoring Rubric.** Evaluate the child's writing one criterion at a time.

- You will often find that a child's writing receives different scores for different criteria. The final score, however, should be a single number. In reaching a holistic score, give the most weight to Genre and to Organization and Focus.

- Analyze each child's errors, using the criteria and the lesson numbers provided. Reteach those lessons for skills that caused the child difficulty.

   Genre (Lesson 104–Lesson 106; Lesson 110)

   Organization and Focus (Lesson 107–Lesson 109)

   Sentence Structure (Lesson 111)

- Provide corrective feedback about errors in grammar, usage, and mechanics. If necessary, consider reteaching lessons in Sections 1–7.

Scoring Rubric

	Informational Paragraph
Score 4	**Genre** The writer tells important facts about a single topic. Exact words help make the facts clear and interesting to read.
	Organization and Focus The topic sentence is precise and clear. Supporting sentences include only facts that tell more about the topic.
	Sentence Structure The writer uses both long and short sentences, as well as different kinds of sentences.
	Conventions There are not many mistakes in grammar, spelling, or punctuation.
Score 3	**Genre** The writer gives information about a single topic. However, he or she may need to include a few more facts. Some words could be more exact.
	Organization and Focus The topic sentence may not be clear. Supporting sentences may include a few facts or other details that do not tell more about the topic.
	Sentence Structure Some of the sentences are short and choppy. The writer could vary sentences more.
	Conventions There are some mistakes but none make the writing hard to understand.
Score 2	**Genre** The writer does not give information about a single topic or does not include facts at all. Many words are vague or unclear.
	Organization and Focus The topic sentence is confusing or misleading. Supporting sentences may include many facts or other details that do not tell more about the topic.
	Sentence Structure Many of the sentences are short and choppy.
	Conventions There are many mistakes. Some make the writing hard to understand.
Score 1	**Genre** The topic is not clear. There are no details. Words are vague or confusing.
	Organization and Focus There is no topic sentence. Supporting sentences are missing.
	Sentence Structure All of the sentences are short and choppy.
	Conventions Mistakes make the writing hard to understand.

Grammar Transfer Issues for Ten Languages

The following chart identifies areas in which speakers of various primary languages may have some difficulty acquiring English grammar (syntax). The type of transfer error and its cause is outlined for each grammatical category.

Nouns

Type of Transfer Error in English	Language Background	Cause of Transfer Difficulty
Plural Forms omission of plural marker -s *I have five book.*	Cantonese, Haitian Creole, Hmong, Khmer, Korean, Tagalog, Vietnamese	Nouns do not change form to show the plural in the primary language.
Possessive Forms avoidance of *'s* to describe possession *the children of my sister* instead of *my sister's children*	Haitian Creole, Hmong, Khmer, Spanish, Tagalog, Vietnamese	Using a prepositional phrase to express possession reflects the only structure or a more common structure in the primary language.
Not Using *'s or s'* no marker for possessive forms *house my friend* instead of *my friend's house*	Haitian Creole, Khmer, Vietnamese	An object's owner comes after the object in the primary language.

Articles

Type of Transfer Error in English	Language Background	Cause of Transfer Difficulty
Omitting Articles *He has job.* *His dream job is to become lawyer, not teacher.*	Cantonese, Haitian Creole, Hmong, Khmer, Korean, Russian, Tagalog, Vietnamese	Either articles are lacking or there is no parallel distinction between *a* and *the* in the primary language.
Overusing Articles *The honesty is the best policy.* *This food is popular in the Japan.* *I like the cats.*	Arabic, Haitian Creole, Hmong, Spanish, Tagalog	An article is used in the primary language in places where it isn't used in English.
Not Using *a/an* use of *one* for *a/an* *He is one engineer.*	Haitian Creole, Hmong, Vietnamese	Learners sometimes confuse the articles *a/an* with *one* since articles either do not exist in the primary language or serve a different function.

Pronouns

Type of Transfer Error in English	Language Background	Cause of Transfer Difficulty
Personal Pronouns, Gender use of pronouns with inappropriate gender *He is my sister.*	Cantonese, Haitian Creole, Hmong, Khmer, Korean, Tagalog	The third-person pronoun in the primary language is gender-free. The same pronoun is used where English uses masculine, feminine, or neuter pronouns, resulting in confusion of pronoun forms in English.

Pronouns (Continued)

Type of Transfer Error in English	Language Background	Cause of Transfer Difficulty
Personal Pronouns, Gender use of pronouns with inappropriate gender *He is my sister.*	Spanish	In Spanish, subject pronouns are dropped in everyday speech and verbs convey third-person agreement, effectively collapsing the two pronouns and causing transfer difficulty with subject pronouns in English.
Personal Pronouns, Gender use of inappropriate gender, particularly with neuter nouns *The house is big. She is beautiful.*	Russian, Spanish	Inanimate nouns have feminine and masculine gender in the primary language, which may be carried over into English.
Personal Pronoun Forms confusion of subject and object pronoun forms *Him hit me. I like she. Let we go.*	Cantonese, Hmong, Khmer	The same pronoun form is used for *he/him* and *she/her*, and in some primary languages for *I/me* and *we/us*.
Number use of incorrect number for pronouns *I saw many yellow flowers. It was pretty.*	Cantonese, Korean	There is no number agreement in the primary language.
Subject Pronouns omission of subject pronouns *Michael isn't here. Is in school.*	Korean, Russian, Spanish	Subject pronouns may be dropped in the primary language, with the verb ending supplying information on number and/or gender.
Object Pronouns omission of object pronouns *That man is very rude, so nobody likes.*	Korean, Vietnamese	Direct objects are frequently dropped in the primary language.
Personal Pronoun Forms use of pronouns with subject nouns *This car, it runs very fast.* *Your friend, he seems so nice.* *My parents, they live in Vietnam.*	Hmong, Vietnamese	This type of redundant structure reflects the popular "topic-comment" approach used in the primary language: The speaker mentions a topic and then makes a comment on it.
Pronoun *one* omission of the pronoun *one* *I saw two nice cars, and I like the small.*	Russian, Spanish, Tagalog	Adjectives can be used on their own in the primary language, whereas English often requires a noun or *one*.
Possessive Forms confusion of possessive forms *The book is my.*	Cantonese, Hmong, Vietnamese	Cantonese and Hmong speakers tend to omit final *n*, creating confusion between *my* and *mine*.

Adjectives

Type of Transfer Error in English	Language Background	Cause of Transfer Difficulty
Word Order: Adjectives position of adjectives after nouns *I read a book interesting.*	Haitian Creole, Hmong, Khmer, Spanish, Vietnamese	Adjectives commonly come after nouns in the primary language.
Word Order: Adjectives position of adjectives before certain pronouns *This is interesting something.*	Cantonese, Korean	Adjectives always come before words they modify in the primary language.

Adjectives (Continued)

Type of Transfer Error in English	Language Background	Cause of Transfer Difficulty
Comparison omission of markers for comparison *She is smart than me.*	Khmer	Since there are no suffixes or inflections in Khmer, the tendency is to omit them in English.
Comparison avoidance of *-er* and *-est* endings *I am more old than my brother.*	Hmong, Khmer, Korean, Spanish	Comparatives and superlatives are usually formed with separate words in the primary language, the equivalent of *more* and *most* in English.
Confusion of *-ing* and *-ed* Forms *The movie was <u>bored</u>.* *I am very <u>interesting</u> in sports.*	Cantonese, Khmer, Korean, Spanish	The adjective forms in the primary language that correspond to those in English do not have active and passive meanings. In Korean, for many adjectives, the same form is used for both active and passive meanings, such as *boring* and *bored*.

Verbs

Type of Transfer Error in English	Language Background	Cause of Transfer Difficulty
Present Tense omission of *s* in present tense, third-person agreement *She <u>go</u> to school every day.*	Cantonese, Haitian Creole, Hmong, Khmer, Korean, Tagalog, Vietnamese	There is no verb agreement in the primary language.
Present Tense problems with irregular subject-verb agreement *Sue and Ed <u>has</u> a new house.*	Cantonese, Hmong, Khmer, Korean, Tagalog	Verb forms do not change to indicate the number of the subject in the primary language.
Past Tense omission of tense markers *I study <u>English</u> yesterday.* *I <u>give</u> it to him yesterday.*	Cantonese, Haitian Creole, Hmong, Khmer, Korean, Tagalog, Vietnamese	Verbs do not change form to express tense in the primary language.
Past Tense confusion of present form and simple past of regular verbs *I <u>give</u> it to him yesterday.*	Cantonese, Spanish	Speakers of the primary language have difficulty recognizing that merely a vowel shift in the middle of the verb, rather than a change in the ending, is sufficient to produce a change of tense in irregular verbs.
Future Tense incorrect use of present for the future *I <u>come</u> tomorrow.*	Cantonese, Korean	The primary language allows use of present tense for the future.
Negative Statements omission of helping verbs in negative statements *I no understand.* *I not get in university.*	Cantonese, Korean, Russian, Spanish, Tagalog	Helping verbs are not used in negative statements in the primary language.
Main Verb omission of main verb *Criticize people not good.*	Cantonese	Unlike English, Cantonese does not require an infinitive marker when using a verb as a noun.

Verbs (Continued)

Type of Transfer Error in English	Language Background	Cause of Transfer Difficulty
Main Verb use of two or more main verbs in one clause without any connectors *I took a book went studied at the library.*	Hmong	In Hmong, verbs can be connected without *and* or any other conjunction (serial verbs).
Linking Verbs omission of linking verb *He hungry.*	Cantonese, Haitian Creole, Hmong, Khmer, Russian, Vietnamese	The verb *be* is not required in all sentences. In some languages, it is implied in the adjective form. In others, the concept is expressed as a verb.
Passive Voice omission of helping verb *be* in passive voice *The food finished.*	Cantonese, Vietnamese	Passive voice in the primary language does not require a helping verb.
have Versus be use of *have* instead of *be* *I have hunger.* *I have right.*	Spanish	Some Spanish constructions use *have* where English uses *be*.

Adverbs

Type of Transfer Error in English	Language Background	Cause of Transfer Difficulty
Omitting Adverbs use of adjective form where adverb form is needed *Walk quiet.*	Haitian Creole, Hmong, Khmer	There are no suffix-derived adverb forms in the primary language, and the adjective form is used after the verb.
Placement placement of adverbs before verbs *At ten o'clock this morning my plane landed.* avoiding the alternate *My plane landed at ten o'clock this morning.*	Cantonese, Korean	Adverbs usually come before verbs in the primary language, and this tendency is carried over into English.

Sentence Structure

Type of Transfer Error in English	Language Background	Cause of Transfer Difficulty
Objects omission of object *He dyed [his hair].* *Yes, I want [some].*	Korean	Korean tends to omit objects and noun phrases after verbs.
Variety lack of variety in the positions of clauses *Because you weren't at home and I couldn't find [you], I left.* avoiding the alternate *I left because you weren't at home and I couldn't find [you].*	Korean	Since main clauses always come last in Korean, there is a tendency to put the main clause last in English. This is not an error in English, but it leads to a lack of sentence variety.
Word Order: Clauses clauses that describe earlier actions come first *After I finish my homework, I will watch TV.* avoiding the alternate *I will watch TV after I finish my homework.*	Cantonese, Korean	The pattern in the primary language is to describe what happens first, followed by later occurrences. This is not an error in English, but it leads to a lack of sentence variety.

Sentence Structure (*Continued*)

Type of Transfer Error in English	Language Background	Cause of Transfer Difficulty
Word Order: Indirect Objects placement of phrase with an indirect object before a direct object *They gave to the girl the book.*	Spanish	A phrase with an indirect object can come before a direct object in Spanish.
Word Order: Modifiers placement of modifiers between verb and direct object *She speaks <u>very well</u> English.*	Korean, Spanish	Word order, including the placement of adverbials, is freer in the primary language than in English.
Double Negatives use of double negatives *I <u>no</u> see <u>nobody</u>.*	Spanish	Spanish requires double negatives in many sentence structures.

Questions

Type of Transfer Error in English	Language Background	Cause of Transfer Difficulty
Word Order: Questions avoidance of English inverted question forms for yes/no questions in favor of tag questions or intonation *You come tomorrow, OK?* *He goes to school with you?*	Cantonese, Haitian Creole, Khmer, Korean, Russian, Tagalog, Vietnamese	The primary language doesn't use subject-verb inversion for questions.
Word Order: Helping Verbs lack of subject-verb inversion for questions with helping verbs *When she will be home?* *Where you are going?*	Cantonese, Hmong, Russian, Tagalog	In the primary language, word order is the same in some questions and statements, depending on the context.
Yes/No Questions incorrect answer forms for yes/no questions *A: Do you want more food?* *B: I want.* *A: Do you have a pen?* *B: I not have.*	Cantonese, Hmong, Khmer, Korean, Russian	In the primary language, learners tend to answer yes by repeating the verb in the question. They tend to say no by using *not* and repeating the verb.
Yes/No Questions omission of *do* or *did* in questions *Where you went?*	Haitian Creole, Hmong, Khmer, Korean, Russian, Spanish, Tagalog	In the primary language, there is no exact counterpart to the *do/did* verb for questions.
Answers positive answers to negative questions *A: Aren't you going?* *B: Yes. (when the person is not going)*	Cantonese, Korean, Russian	The appropriate response pattern differs between the primary language and English.
Tag Questions incorrect tag questions *You want to go home, are you?*	Cantonese, Khmer, Korean, Vietnamese	The primary language has no exact counterpart to a tag question, forms them differently, or does not add *do/did* to questions.